D1628002

THE GROWTH OF BRITISH EDUCATION AND ITS RECORDS

Colin R Chapman

SECOND EDITION

LOCHIN PUBLISHING

This is another in the series of Chapmans Records Cameos designed to bring some of the less often used record sources to the attention of social, local and family historians world-wide. This Cameo and others in the series by the author originated as his lectures, many of which are profusely illustrated with pertinent examples. The author will, accordingly, be pleased to lecture to family history, genealogical or other societies or groups on the subject of this Cameo or other matters of interest to the social, local and family historian.

The cover illustration is adapted by Sarah Elliott from Thomas Webster's 'A Dame School' of 1845, to which reference is made in Chapter 6.

Published by
LOCHIN PUBLISHING
6 Holywell Road, Dursley, GL11 5RS, England

First Edition 1991 (1 873686 01 3)
Second (revised) Edition 1992
Reprinted 1996
Copyright of the Lochin Publishing Society 1991, 1992

British Library Cataloguing in Publication Data
Chapman, Colin, 1939-
The Growth of British Education and its Records - 2 Rev. ed.
(Chapmans Records Cameos Series)
I. Title II. Elliott, Sarah III.Series
379.0941
ISBN 1 873686 05 6

Table of Contents

Preface

Very many years ago I was a student in London; being a keen young organist I attended, on most Sundays, the Temple Church - the private chapel of the Benchers of the Inner Temple. Not only did I have the opportunity to be guided musically by Dr George Thalben-Ball, and to get to know the choir, but I also gained some understanding of the roles and histories over the centuries of the Inns of Court and Chancery.

Not so many years ago, while being trained as a teacher in further education, I was compelled to study the History of Education in England and Wales. I emphasise "compelled" as there was an examination at the conclusion of the course and accordingly my attention was held with some compulsion. Notwithstanding, I was fascinated by the development of various academies of learning and schools of teaching and to me the topic became more than a mere module of information I had to absorb and regurgitate during the appropriate assessment.

A few years ago my professional work took me to the Army School of Instructional Technology and to the Royal Naval School at Greenwich to exchange experiences in techniques of instruction and assessment. It was evident that the methods employed by the army and also by the Senior Service had evolved over very many decades, even centuries, and I began to ferret into the history and development of education and training within each of the armed services.

More recently I was invited to the Newberry Library in Chicago to present a seminar on English Genealogical Research; whilst there I was privileged to be taken through the stacks (it is not an "open library") and I stumbled across a book of essays written by an ancestor of mine, George Brimley, while he was Librarian of Trinity College, Cambridge and so associated with St Augustine (see Chapter 2) a millenium and a half ago. Back in England the present Librarian was extraordinarily helpful in unearthing some marvellous personal notes written by Brimley; these have been retained in the library archives, and gave me a glimpse of a side of his character not evident in his formal prose. But for those notes that aspect of his personality would have been hidden for ever.

Even more recently in the Bedfordshire Record Office I was browsing through the Harrold Village School Log Book for 1885; there, in black and white, for 26 October, was the record of my grandmother, as a little girl, being "suspended on account of parents, who refuse their child to submit to discipline, and on account of the mother threatening personal violence". How I wish she had been alive when I discovered this incident from her past - but I doubt if I would have had the courage to tell her.

It seems only yesterday that I moved home; in emptying some drawers I rediscovered my school report books, my swimming certificates, my English Literature Prize, my hobbies awards, my school annual form photographs taken over eleven years and printed class lists to accompany them, my music reports and dozens of examination certificates. Unwittingly I had assembled - and naturally retained, as to discard anything is alien to my nature - a host of my own pupil-based education records.

It was only yesterday that I was asked to present some papers in Heidelberg. This was a golden opportunity as for some years I had been pursuing the origins and fortunes of an English school which had been founded there in 1887. There had been a strong English community in Heidelberg since the 1820s. The school is now a German academy but in its original premises, unfortunately raped of many of its fittings by billeted servicemen. Nevertheless the Headmaster allowed me to study a scrapbook of newspaper cuttings from the turn of the century and to photograph awards and trophies bedecked with the names of former English pupils from its foundation to the First World War.

Today I had an opportunity to visit the Scottish Record Office in Edinburgh. Whilst there I was able to examine a number of archives relating to education in that part of the British Isles. I can never suppress my excitement in passing on details of source material, after studying the original documentation.

Tomorrow I shall be attending the Award Ceremony for graduands of the University of the West of England (formerly Bristol Polytechnic). Being on the Science Advisory Committee I have received invitations annually for several years; at each ceremony I have been given a commemorative programme with names of the students who have attained their degrees and diplomas, and indicating the subjects in which they have been successful. As each student has an identical programme it could be argued that all are establishment-based records of educational achievement.

It was, therefore, with some inside knowledge that I responded to a request to present a lecture initially on school records and then on those of other educational establishments in the British Isles; and later to demonstrate the value of such records to the family historian and the genealogist, and also to the social historian and the biographer. This cameo derives its pedigree from that lecture and its successors. It has been amplified thanks to the contributions from many members of my audiences who, over the years, have given me snippets of information or who asked questions which caused me to undertake further research. Colleagues on the Council of the Association of Educational and Training Technology have been invaluable in putting me in touch with various sources, custodians and librarians, all of whom were most charming with their assistance. To Professor Duncan Harris of Brunel University who, when at the University of Bath encouraged me to embark on a Masters Degree in Education, I offer particular thanks for immersing me in the world of education and the records which it has generated for centuries.

As Latin has been so well integrated into the growth of education in the British Isles, I believe that my readers will accept my licence in the choice of titles, taken from my school days, for the opening and closing chapters of this cameo.

In this Second Edition I have totally revised Chapters 2 and 3 and included more on Nonconformist and Catholic education; I have added considerably to Chapters 4 and 7 but in doing so have had to sacrifice most illustrations. I believe that the re-written Chapters 13 and 14 and the additions to Chapters 5 and 6 will make this Cameo more attractive to those with Scottish and Irish interests. To those I have thanked previously I must add many others for their generous reviews and also others for information that I have incorporated in this edition.

COLIN R CHAPMAN

Apothecaries, physicians and surgeons, as well as schoolmasters (see Chapter 3) had to obtain a licence from the bishop before they could practise legally. The education and training for these skills, as is typified by this anatomy lesson, was initially provided through the craft guilds (see Chapter 5) such as the Barber Surgeons' Company, out of which grew some of the medical professional bodies referred to in Chapter 10; later the universities (see Chapters 4, 13 and 14) offered medical degrees.

1. Salvete

Many social and family historians, biographers and genealogists have not undertaken detailed research among British education records in the mistaken beliefs that such documents begin after the 1870 Education Act for England and Wales (1872 for Scotland) and that they are denied access to later material. Neither of these beliefs is correct and many education documents in the British Isles can be consulted which were originally written many hundreds of years ago. Indeed, the Irish educational material furnishes a substitute for vital information that was lost by the destruction of civil records in this century. No attempt has been made here to provide a comprehensive history or a commentary on the social impact of British education; there are many volumes which deal adequately with these aspects in considerable detail. Rather, documents emanating from the educational system are identified and the growth of British education is used as a convenient framework on which to adorn that material. Hence the following chapters of this Cameo outline the education provided in England, Wales, Scotland and Ireland and consider some of the material available from the earliest education records until the effects of the Education Acts at the beginning of this century.

Bibliographic references and addresses of repositories holding education records appear in the main text of the following chapters; a judicious use of the Index will enable this information to be easily found. The Table of Contents will enable broad eras and areas of educational interest to be located in the chapters which follow, whilst the Index provides types and names of educational institutions and supporting bodies, not immediately obvious from the chapter titles. Thus for detailed information on English, Welsh, Scottish or Irish education records readers are invited to enjoy the entire text of this Cameo.

"The Educational Question."

2. Early Education in the British Isles

There are no primary documents from educational establishments in the British Isles prior to the seventh century; but from secondary manuscript and archaeological sources it is evident that schooling was being provided very much earlier. In about 380 Ninian, the son of a Cumberland prince, travelled to Rome to study. He returned to the British Isles at the beginning of the fifth century and set up an episcopal college and school for local children at Whitherne in Galloway, Scotland. The Book of Sentences - selections from the Fathers - was written by Ninian for the use of his students. Around this time Pelagius, a Briton, was proclaiming such outragous heretical doctrines in South Britain that in 429 Pope Celestine sent the Gallican bishops Germanus and Lupus as his legates to found schools for both laity and clergy and suppress the hersey. (Incidently, while Germanus was still at Auxerre in Gaul in 418 one of his pupils was Patrick - better known as St Patrick of Ireland). Beginning at Caerleon, the contemporary British capital, the legates erected monastic schools across Britain in which many notable historians and leaders were educated. Some romantics even quote Germanus as sowing the seeds for Oxford and Cambridge universities.

In 430 Celestine consecrated Palladius as bishop "over the Scots believing in Christ" and sent him initially to Ireland. Although Palladius built at least three churches in which he deposited some sacred books and his own writing tablets, the Irish princes were not very hospitable and he moved to Scotland where he established episcopal colleges, schools and seminaries. One of the products of a Scottish education was the good looking and popular Bishop Kentigern who later moved to Wales and erected a school at Llan-Elwy near the Clwyd river. From here missionaries and teachers went to Norway, Iceland and the Orkney islands. His favourite scholar, Asaph gave his name to the surrounding diocese. Also in Wales, Cadoc, son of a Brecknockshire prince, was educated for 12 years at Gwent College in Monmouthshire, where he was tutored by Tathai, an Irish teacher. Cadoc subsequently founded

Llancarvan School near Cowbridge in Glamorganshire.

When St Patrick returned to Ireland, besides his itinerant teaching of Latin and the Scriptures, he established an episcopal monastery and a school at Armagh, if not others, in which Benignus and Gildas subsequently taught; this school later (in the eighth century) received financial support from Irish kings. Bishop Nicholson commented that within a century of the death of St Patrick "the Irish Seminaries had so increased that most parts of Europe sent their children to be educated here, and drew thence their bishops and teachers". One of the earliest monastic schools was erected around 480 by Prince Enda of Orgiel on the Isle of Aran, off the west coast of Ireland. St Carthag the Elder, St Kieran, St Brendan (who later founded Clonfert School in Connaught) and St Fursey were educated at the Aran school. At Clonard School, founded in Westmeath by St Finian around 540, many saints and doctors, including St Columba, received their initial schooling. Benchor monastery, founded near Carrickfergus in 559 by St Comgall, produced famous leaders such as St Columbanus (who founded Luxeuil in Burgundy in 585) and Luanus, who later travelled across Europe setting up schools, monasteries and centres of learning in Gaul, Germany, Switzerland, Bavaria, and Italy. St Columba, from Clonard School, went on to found Iona in 563 really as a Missionary College to educate those who were later to take education and Christianity from the north-west to the heathen Picts, Scots, Welsh and Britons.

Coming from the south-east, the Christian missionary, Augustine, was sent to England by Pope Gregory I in 597; the inventory of the books that Augustine carried is preserved at Trinity College, Cambridge: a two-volume Bible, a Psalter, a book of the Gospels, a Martyrology, the Apocryphal Lives of the Apostles, and the Exposition of certain Epistles and Gospels. The inventory concludes "These are the foundation or beginning of the library of the whole English Church" . Within a century of Augustine converting the Saxon kingdom of Kent, Archbishop Theodore and Abbot Adrian had established what were much later renamed King's School at Canterbury and King's School at Rochester, both in Kent. Some authorities believe that an even earlier school had been connected with Malmesbury Abbey in Wiltshire in the fifth century, but this has not survived in almost unbroken descent to the present, as have those in Kent. Archbishop Theodore was also responsible for dividing the country into ecclesiastical bishoprics or dioceses which subsequently proved useful when the Church was administering education (and other social philanthropy) as well as religion. Leading ecclesiastics moved on from Canterbury up to York in 627 where St Peter's School was founded and then on to Northumbria in 674 where the famous library at Jarrow was established in the Monastery in 682. Bede's great works of history and scholarship were enhanced through his access to the Jarrow library built up with books from Ireland, the European Continent and Rome. On Iona the students were studying the classics, mechanical arts, law, history, physic, husbandry, horticulture and the blacksmith's trade. St Columba himself hand-wrote the Book of Kells, now preserved at Trinity College, Dublin. Penmanship and poetry appear to have been specialities of early Irish education: many classical texts were illustrated by Irish scholars while Irish poets were renowned across Europe, often accompanying their poetry with music on the harp.

Cathedral Schools were established as the Christian Church expanded in the British Isles, and by the ninth century York had become as notable as Canterbury. The school at Armagh by this time boasted 7000 students and the country around Leighlin was known as the "land of saints and scholars"; and although the Danes repeatedly attacked Ireland in this and the tenth centuries the succession of Professors of Divinity was maintained and has been documented by Usher. Originally the function of the Cathedral Schools was to train the clergy, but they also provided education in spiritual, temporal and commercial affairs for the sons of the nobility. As Latin was at that time the language of the Church it was necessary to have schools to teach at least this subject to the newly-converted clerics. The schools were normally small, having less than a hundred boys, but of exceptional quality; those at Raithin and Lismore, founded in Ireland by St Carthag the Younger in the seventh century are typical.

While the noble classes could find suitable centres of learning for their sons, others were less fortunate and educational standards generally in England began to decline, particularly following the intrusions of heathen Danes. Alfred the Great, conscious of this problem attempted in 880 to improve the accessibility of educational opportunities by encouraging the teaching and reading of English throughout the country. In the late tenth century the Benedictine monk Aelfric compiled very many school books including a Latin vocabulary and grammar in Anglo-Saxon to help the young monks in the reformed monastery schools. Outside the monasteries it is probable that whatever teaching was available was conducted on a tutorial basis and in the pupils' homes.

3. The Church and Education

In common with most aspects of life in the British Isles, attempts to improve learning and understanding, not only in the early days, as described in Chapter 2 above, but for many centuries were often introduced directly by the Church or by benefactors linked with the Church. For example Gilbert, rector of Sempringham in Lincolnshire in about 1120, kept a school for the village children, while in Aberdeen in 1124 and in Stirling in 1173 schools were linked to the monasteries and cathedrals. Even in the eleventh century, Bishop Sulgenus of St David's had spent ten years studying in Irish monastic schools.

Apart from direct instruction from the priests, schools for local boys were attached to many chantries across the country towards the end of the Middle Ages; a founder provided an endowment not only to build the chantry in or near the church to house his tomb but also to maintain clerics (magistri scolara) to celebrate masses for his soul and teach the boys. Whereas the temporal authorities may have been reactive in providing educational establishments it was frequently ecclesiastics who took a proactive role and those intimately connected with the Church who were chosen as teachers and tutors. Indeed, the Council of Westminster in 1200 confirmed the eleventh Canon of the Third Lateran Council that "he who taught in the bishop's church should be approved of by the bishop". It was on this philosophy that subsequent cases (eg that of Gloucester Grammar School in 1410) brought before the ecclesiastical courts against non- approved schoolmasters were based. Later injunctions reinforced this concept (in 1555 for example, "that schoolmasters of any sort be not admitted till they be by their Ordinary examined and allowed"). An Ordinary was defined as a more senior or superior cleric, usually a bishop; some of the "examinations" were in practice reviews by an ecclesiastical court and those who were "allowed" to teach were the successful applicants - as is fully explained in the Chapmans Records Cameo 'Ecclesiastical Courts, their Officials and their Records', published by Lochin. In the Glasgow diocese a priest was forced to close his school in 1494 because he was teaching without the bishop's approval. Actual teaching licences, see below, were introduced a century later.

Several factors influenced this situation which reinforced the interwoven complexities of government by both Church and State; there was the import- ance placed on religion in the spiritual and social life of the British Isles, the unquestioned premise that religion was fundamental to all education, the nationwide organisation and hierarchical structure of the Church with its access to considerable wealth, the importance of Latin in secular as well as ecclesiastical documentation and the very instructional nature of an incum- bent's daily routine whose teaching skills were as important as his pastoral duties. It should not be overlooked that prior to 1534 the Church in England was the Church of Rome and not until after then did it become the Protestant Church of England with strong Protestant connections with the Church of Ireland and to a lesser extent with the Church of Scotland.

Even after Henry VIII had closed the monasteries from 1546 and the chantries from 1548 (and so their schools), and had begun to sell them off - a pattern which continued under Edward VI - the cash so realised was invested back into educational foundations, such as the King's Schools, linked to the Church. Following the Reformation in England, when the Church and the Monarchy became almost indistinguishable - indeed so much so that the pendulum of Protestantism swung to Puritanism and then into Civil War - schools were used as a vehicle to promote anti-Roman beliefs; how this was circumvented in Ireland is described in Chapters 5 and 7 below. John Knox's proposals on a school-building programme in Scotland at this time are outlined in Chapter 13.

Among the 140 or so Canons prepared in 1603, which came into force in 1604 to improve the structure and effectiveness of the Reformed Church, one (number 77) required a schoolmaster to hold an actual licence to teach; whilst another (number 137) required the licence to be produced at the Bishop's Visitation. Such licences were issued by the bishops or their representatives through the ecclesiastical courts. Furthermore, the schoolmasters as well as the clergy had to subscribe to the Thirty Nine Articles to ensure that no Popery was promulgated through the education system. The bishops' licences were required before legally teaching in any school, whether attached to an ecclesiastical body, a private institution or a public body, although it seems to have applied mainly in grammar or endowed schools rather than smaller village institutions. This, of course, did not prevent many unlicensed school-masters from teaching quite illegally. Licensing of schoolteachers was for-mally abolished in 1869 under the Endowed Schools Act but there are isolated examples of licences being issued in the present century. In the army, even in the eighteenth century, schoolmasters were picked with strong Protestant backgrounds to ensure they would not be swayed by Catholic influence.

Many village schools did not have their own premises and so the pupils were accommodated in the parish church, obviously influencing the teaching proffered, especially if the teacher was the parish priest himself. At many a parish church the school was conducted in a room over the south porch - in fact not a few porches were built with a room above in which to specifically house the parish library and teach the scholars of the village. This accounts for the name parvise given to this porch by the Victorians; although the word strictly means paradise (not always appropriate for a schoolroom) it was also used in the fifteenth century to denote a room, and hence a porch with a room above it. In the diocese of Carlisle the Bishop's Visitation of 1702 revealed that schools were being held in a fifth of the 101 churches. To this day some church walls bear the evidence of being used to portray visual aids: there is a multiplication table at Long Melford in Suffolk and two alphabets at North Cadbury in Somerset.

The Society for Promoting Christian Knowledge (SPCK), an Anglican organisation, was foremost in aiding the foundation of parochial schools from the late seventeenth century, further cementing the ties between the Church and education. Many collections taken during Church services were specifi-cally towards the education of the local children. In the nineteenth century the Established Church supported the activities of Rev Andrew Bell in the National Schools (see Chapter 7 below); in fact the parochial, archidiaconal and diocesan structure of the Church enabled these schools to spread throug-hout the country.

However, it was not only the Established Church that was concerned for the education of children and adults. As described above, immediately following the Reformation only teachers loyal to the Anglican Church were permitted to practise. But after the Declaration of Indulgence in 1672 and the Toleration Act of 1689 some nonconformists were permitted to exercise (within certain constraints) their particular religious beliefs and they began to establish their own academic centres.

Jews and Quakers were among the first groups to be tolerated and both supported their own charity schools: the Gates of Hope Charity School for Educating and Apprenticing Forty Boys was opened in London for children of Spanish and Portuguese (Sephardi) Jews in 1664, although English was not introduced until 1736. A Villareal School for Girls, at which the teaching was in English, was opened in 1731. In 1732 a (Ashkenazim) Jewish charity, Talmud Torah, was founded to which an Orphan Charity School was attached. This changed its name in 1814 to the Free School for German Jews at which the teaching followed the monitorial systems of Bell and Lancaster. In 1807 the London Missionary Society established a Free School for Jewish Boys and Girls in an attempt to convert them to the Christian faith, as well as provide education. The London Society for Promoting Christianity Among Jews was set up with similar missionary aims, and further schools were opened in the East End of London in 1811, 1812 and 1813. The Quakers took an interest, and continue to do so, in the education of adults as well as children. Many of their educational establishments and their records are described in subsequent chapters.

Independents (becoming Congregationalists), Baptists, Presbyterians, Moravians and later Methodists and even Unitarians, and in the nineteenth century many other denominations and religious groups who may be described as Church communities or congregations established schools for their adherents and their children. Ashley J W Smith's 'Birth of Modern Education: the Contribution of the Dissenting Academies, 1660-1800' published by the Independent Press in 1954 has details on some of these groups.

Roman Catholics were not so readily tolerated in England, Wales and Scotland and they generally had to seek their education elsewhere until the nineteenth century. A list of Catholic schools offering education at this time was published in 1845 - see Chapter 11 below. A Catholic Poor School Committee was established in 1847 by the eight Vicars Apostolic of the Catholic Church in England and Wales to provide religious (Catholic) education for children of the poor. There is no doubt that this was a missionary effort to bring converts into the Catholic faith, in the same way that the Christian schools for Jewish children were seeking their souls for Christ; and there was considerable anti-Roman debate, for example in the English Review of 1849, against the State encouraging "this form of Romish activity", but at least more poor children were being given a chance to receive some education even if biased. However, Seminaries in Continental Europe, such as those listed in Guilday's 'English Catholics on the Continent', had been providing schooling, especially for British Catholic girls for very many years. Further details on Catholic schooling may be found in Michael Gandy's 'My Ancestors were Catholics' published by the Society of Genealogists.

Nevertheless, the strong links between the Established Church and the State continued into the twentieth century, and even today the Church has a strong influence on educational curricula and standards in the British Isles. Many of the above examples are expanded further in the appropriate chapters below.

4. British University and Tertiary Education

The University of Oxford was founded as an offshoot of Paris University around 1167; in 1209 a breakaway group moved from Oxford to Cambridge to join some young academics who had settled there in 1112, so establishing that famous institution. These Universities, which remained the only two in England until Durham was founded in 1832, were unique in having no cathedral chancellor - unlike their European counterparts. The institution of colleges, the first being University College at Oxford by 1249 and Peterhouse at Cambridge in 1284, was uniquely English and designed for the benefit of the secular clergy.

There had been, very briefly, another university in England in the thirteenth century following some violence at Oxford and discontent at Cambridge. Aggrieved students left both cities and settled in Northampton in 1238. A formal university was established with approval from Henry III who believed that the university would improve the town. It appeared to have everything in its favour, as the seventeenth century historian Thomas Fuller commended: "their judgment in choice of so convenient a place, where the air is clear, and not over sharp; the earth fruitful, yet not over dirty; water plentiful, yet far from any fennish annoyance; and wood conveniently sufficient in that age. But the main is, Northampton is near the centre of England; so that all travellers coming thither from the remotest parts of the land, may be said to meet by the town in the midst of their journey, so impartial is the situation of it in the navel of the Kingdom". However, nearby Oxford became quite apprehensive at the growing success of Northampton University and persuaded the King to close it by letters patent in 1262. No records of the graduates appear to have survived and many works on English universities totally ignore its existence.

Scottish students seeking tertiary education prior to the fifteenth century had to travel to England (Balliol College, Oxford had been specifically founded for Scots) or even further afield. The records of Bologna, Geneva, Louvain,

Padva, Paris and Pisa universities have many Scottish undergraduates. A Scots College was founded in Paris in 1326 by the Bishop of Moray. But under a Bull of Pope Benedict XIII St Andrew's University, modelled on that at Paris, was founded in 1411; initially there were no colleges and the students lived in the city and were divided into "nations", Fife, Lothian and Angus according to their homes. Any from elsewhere were allocated to the Alban nation. The University of Glasgow, modelled on Louvain, was established in 1450 under a Bull of Pope Nicholas V. Aberdeen University was a later amalgam between King's College (founded in the city in 1494 under a Bull of Pope Alexander VI) and Marischal College (founded in 1593). Edinburgh University was founded in 1583 as the College of Edinburgh and in 1631 granted the rights and privileges of other Scottish Universities. The Scots College in Spain was founded in 1627 for totally different reasons - those of religious persecution, as explained below.

In Ireland Trinity College Dublin was founded in 1591 as a Protestant university on the site of the confiscated monastery of All Hallows in the centre of the city, even though the students may be predominently Roman Catholic today; it should be remembered that the Established Church in Ireland was Anglican (and so committed to the Church of England) until 1870. The National University of Ireland was originally incorporated as Queen's University in 1850 with colleges in Belfast, Cork and Galway (all founded in 1845), becoming the Royal University of Ireland in 1880. In 1908 the Belfast College became the separate Queen's University, Belfast while Cork and Galway were joined by St Patrick's College, Maynooth (founded 1795) and the Catholic University of Ireland (founded 1851) to become the National University with headquarters on the outskirts of Dublin city.

In 1231 Henry III commanded that all students at Oxford and Cambridge should have their names entered on the roll of a particular lecturer, but the earliest of these documents do not appear to have survived. In the thirteenth and fourteenth centuries the majority of the university students were 14 and 15 year old sons of the gentry and merchants, cousins and nephews of successful ecclesiastics or local lads who had demonstrated some initiative. Later records of those who attended these two universities have been published and are available in major public reference libraries throughout the British Isles and in many university libraries elsewhere in the English-speaking world; such alumni records include the dates of the students' admission or matriculation and dates of attaining their degrees, while some have additional biographical and genealogical notes.

'Alumni Oxonienses', edited by Joseph Foster in 1891-92, covers 1500 to 1714 in four volumes although he had previously produced, in 1887-88, a series of four volumes covering the period 1715 to 1886. In 1893 Foster produced two additional volumes which he entitled 'Oxford Men' and 'Oxford Men and their Colleges', covering the period 1880 to 1892 in greater detail and wonderfully illustrated with photographs and engravings. In 1900, 1934 and 1951 editions of an 'Historical Register' with various supplements were published to bring the work of Foster up to date. In 1959 A B Emden completed three volumes of 'A Biographical Register of the University of Oxford to AD 1500'; for many of the students these volumes furnish considerably more information than Foster's research.

The first attempt at Cambridge to provide some details on the students began in 1858 when Charles Henry Cooper, with his eldest son Thompson Cooper, published volume one of 'Athenae Cantabrigienses 1500-1585'. Three years later volume two for the period 1586-1609 was published, although their considerable research had taken the enterprise to 1611. It was not until 1913 that the final two years were published as volume three, incorporating an index for the whole period compiled by George J Gray. This work was largely superseded by 'Alumni Cantabrigienses' for the period until 1751, edited by John and John Archibald Venn, and a second series from 1752 to 1900, edited by the former. Both these series give more details on the scholars than Foster's Oxford series: the Venns' works often include names of wives, dates of death and greater genealogical data. In 1963 A B Emden prepared 'A Biographical Register of the University of Cambridge to 1500' as a companion to his Oxford work. As with the Oxford Register his Cambridge volume contains more details than those of other editors and, indeed, a number of students not before identified.

For both the Oxford and the Cambridge series it is advisable to verify and amplify the particulars with the universities and the colleges themselves. Some college admission registers state the names of the freshmen's former schools or tutors, even in the seventeenth century - thereby providing the biographer and genealogist with additional data and pointing the way to further sources to research. Information on scholars from the other universities in England such as Durham, London (1836), or Bristol (1876) and from those in Scotland and Ireland can be obtained from published registers (similar to the Alumni series) or from the university authorities concerned.

It is useful to remember that until 1871 Oxford, Cambridge and Durham admitted only those loyal to the Established Church, and so no dissenters will be found in the records of these universities before that time. It should also be remembered, as mentioned above in Chapter 3, that prior to 1534 the Established Church was Roman Catholic and thus dissenters before that date would have included all "protesters". Hence those attending the English universities before the Reformation would most likely have been at least nominally of the Catholic faith, and others seeking this type of education would have had private tutors, in some cases outside of Britain. For the opposite reason Roman Catholics and all others after the Reformation who did not conform to the Established faith (Quakers, Jews and other dissenters), would have attended European universities or English academies in Europe if they required education at this level. The English Colleges at Rome, Valladolid and Lisbon, Douai College in France (founded in 1568 and closed in 1794), St Omers, Bruges and Liege College in Spanish Flanders and the Austrian Netherlands (from 1593 to 1794), and the Scots College in Spain (founded in 1627 and still flourishing) are examples of some European academic centres where alternative education was provided for English and Scottish students. Fortunately for genealogists the registers, diaries and other documentation from many of these academies have been transcribed, in some cases translated, and published independently or by bodies such as the Catholic Record Society.

On the other hand, London was established specifically as a non- sectarian university in 1836. London University was also the first in England to admit women to its degrees - in 1878. Women were not admitted at Oxford until 1920 or at Cambridge until 1923 for degrees, although colleges had been founded at Cambridge (Girton in 1869 and Newnham in 1871) for women to attend for honours examinations. Very often father and son, and sometimes grandson, attended the same university or even the same college while brothers and cousins abound in the published material of British universities.

Some colleges, originally set up by local benefactors or communities, such as Owen's College in Manchester (1851) and the Yorkshire College of

Science in Leeds (1874), have subsequently attained the status of university although initially their students took external degrees from the University of London. Some University Extension Colleges were opened (at Exeter and Nottingham, for example) which later also became universities in their own right. Many of these establishments have published alumni lists of their students, a number with most useful biographical details. Polytechnics, though normally associated with post-war tertiary British education, originated in the nineteenth century. The Regent Street Polytechnic in London was founded in 1882 and by 1897 there were eight others all funded by local government authorities. Some, similarly to the nineteenth century colleges in Manchester and Leeds, have subsequently either become universities or at least been able to award degrees and many have published lists of students. Stirling University was erected in 1967, after a gap of four centuries in the Scottish tertiary education building programme.

A petition to Rome in 1406 for universities to be founded in the north and south of Wales failed, as did a request during the Commonwealth period for a university in Shrewsbury for Welsh students. Many Welshmen attended Jesus College at Oxford, which had been founded in 1573 by Dr Hugh Price of Brecon; but there was nothing for Welsh nonconformists, even when St David's College was chartered at Lampeter in 1828 and began offering Bachelors' degrees in 1865 - it was too closely allied to the Anglican Church. Not until University College opened at Aberystwyth in 1872 (in a failed hotel) were all denominations in Wales able to receive tertiary education in a Welsh institution. Initially the students took external degrees from the University of London, as they also did at similar colleges in Cardiff from 1883 and Bangor from 1884. However, in 1893 the University of Wales was created from these three colleges with government financial support from London but awarding its own degrees. There are registers from these and four other Welsh colleges, including St David's, which later joined the University of Wales between 1920 and 1969.

An extremely helpful and comprehensive list of 'Registers of the Universities, Colleges and Schools of Great Britain and Ireland' was compiled in 1964 by Dr Phyllis Jacobs and published by the Athlone Press.

Although not strictly universities, the Inns of Court and the Inns of Chancery were the English academies providing tertiary education in law. These Inns were established out of necessity as neither Oxford nor Cambridge formally recognised the study of common law until as late as the mid-nineteenth century. In the early days academic lawyers studied only civil and canon law, and even the latter was forbidden at the Reformation in 1535. It is, therefore, understandable that in 1615 Sir George Buc described these law academies as the "Third University of England". Many sons of gentlemen attended the Inns, not necessarily to become lawyers but to learn the rudiments of English law and also "exercises of manhood, of ornament and delicacy, of learning and activity" to enable them to better manage, defend and extend their estates and to demonstrate the qualities of "real" gentlemen. Much of the learning technique at the Inns of Court and Chancery included participation in "mootings" or mock debates or hearings of various legal processes. The Inns not only provided rooms for these mootings but halls for both informal and very formal dining and accommodation for the students. As their activities developed over the centuries the Inns of Court became societies of barristers whereas the Inns of Chancery were societies of attorneys and solicitors. Today there are four Inns of Court - Inner Temple, Middle Temple, Gray's and Lincoln's. However, in the sixteenth century, although many students went direct to one of the four just mentioned, they were expected to study at an Inn of Chancery before an Inn of Court. As a result there was an association between each Inn of Court and particular Inns of Chancery - for example an Inn of Court sent a Reader to conduct and supervise the legal education at "its" Inn of Chancery. Under the wing of the Inner Temple came Clifford's, Clement's and Lloyd's Inns, under the Middle Temple came Chester (later Strand) Inn and New Inn, under Lincoln's came Furnival's and Davy's (or Thavies') Inns and under Gray's came Staple and Barnard's Inns. There were also some wholly independent Inn's of Chancery, namely two Serjeants' Inns and a Dane's Inn, Scroope's Inn (which was junior to Serjeants' Inn) and St George's Inn.

The meeting "to consult the affairs of the House" was termed a Parliament at the Inner and Middle Temples, a Council at Lincoln's Inn and a Pension at Gray's Inn. The associated Inn of Chancery generally used the same terminology, but Clement's Inn called their assembly a Pension , and recorded their business in a Pension Book. The Clement's Inn Pension Book from 1714 to 1750 was transcribed and published in 1960 by the Selden Society; a list of Members admitted to Clement's Inn from 1656 to 1883, transcribed from two Admissions Books in the Public Record Office, was included in this book. The Inns of Court likewise maintained records of their students and also records of decisions of their Benchers (the senior lawyers). The students' records often included their fathers' names, residences and sometimes greater biographical details. The Sub-Treasurer, Under- Treasurer or Librarian of the appropriate Inn of Court should be approached in writing to obtain details from their records although all Inns have published material which is available in the larger public or university reference libraries. The books to consult are 'Students Admitted to the Inner Temple, 1547-1660', the three volume 'Middle Temple Admissions Register 1501-1944' and the Lincoln's Inn 'Admissions Register 1420-1893' in two volumes. The 'Register of Admissions to Gray's Inn 1521-1889' most usefully includes marriages which took place in the Gray's Inn Chapel between 1695 and 1754. Other books, such as 'The Inner Temple: its Early history as Illustrated by its Records 1505- 1603' by F A Inderwick in 1896, are full of names of students and staff; many, such as Inderwick's volume, have very full indexes.

The senior lawyers' deliberations are not so readily available but the respective libraries or Treasurer's offices of the Inns of Court have copies of their own books, similar to the Clement's Inn Pension Book referred to above. These are called 'Bench Books' for the Inner Temple, 'Benchers' Books' for the Middle Temple, 'Black Books' for Lincoln's Inn and 'Pension Books' for Gray's Inn. Most of these Benchers' records contain references to individual students, in some cases back to the foundation of the Inn, and are thus worthy of consultation.

The Inns of Chancery gradually lost their popularity such that by the eighteenth century even at the surviving Inns the mootings had already died out at several of them and by the nineteenth century only Clement's Inn continued the practice. At this time there was a proposal to amalgamate the remaining Inns of Chancery into a legal university for potential solicitors. However, this idea was dismissed by a Royal Commission in 1854. The last Inn of Chancery (Clifford's Inn) was sold in 1903 and £77,000 of the sale price of £100,000 was allocated to legal education. Thus at its demise one of the original objectives of these Inns was to be achieved in perpetuity. The addresses of the surviving law academies, the Inns of Court, may be found in current London telephone directories.

In Ireland Collett's Inn had been established outside the walls of the city of Dublin in the time of Edward I to mirror the English law academies. This was forced to move in the reign of Edward III following an arson attack and was re-housed as Preston's Inn. In 1542 this Inn was moved yet again, this time by Henry VIII into the confiscated monastery of Friars' Preachers and renamed King's Inns in his honour. A similar, but not truly equivalent law academy in Scotland was the Faculty of Advocates in Edinburgh, formed after the Scots Act of 1532.

Doctors' Commons is often associated with the Inns of Court and Chancery but in the context of education any association is misplaced: in the late fifteenth century Doctors' Commons was a Society or club of advocates - ecclesiastical lawyers with a doctor's degree - which met in a house near St Paul's Cathedral, London. Later the building, and then the courts in which the advocates practised and also the whole neighbourhood where the officers of the courts were housed, came to be called Doctors' Commons. Thus no formal teaching took place there, and as the lawyers had received their education at Oxford, Cambridge or European universities notably in Italy, further elaboration is inappropriate here. However, Doctors' Commons, the activities of advocates and the courts in which they practised are fully explained in the Chapmans Records Cameo 'Ecclesiastical Courts, their Officials and their Records', published by Lochin.

5. Fourteenth to Sixteenth Century School Developments

In the early fourteenth century some cathedral schools offered scholarships to boys of at least 10 years old who could sing and read. Their education, board and lodging were paid by the almoner, a monastic officer normally responsible for distributing alms to the poor; thus these monastic charity schools are often termed Almonry Schools. The boys sang in the Cathedral choir and acted as page boys to the monks while receiving their education from the secular clerks of the monastery. As one of their duties was to carry faggots of firewood for the monks on chilly nights these young pupils were termed "faggot-carriers" or "fags"; this term was later applied to young boys who undertook similar duties for senior pupils at certain schools.

In most mediaeval schools the boys attended throughout their student lives. There were no vacations as there are today, breaks from study were provided on major Saints' Days - although the highlights were those of St Nicholas (6 December) and Shrove Tuesday. On St Nicholas' Day a boy-bishop was selected who preached a sermon in the local church whereas Shrove Tuesday was a complete holiday with all the boys taking part in the pleasures and sport of the time. The ritual of electing a boy-bishop - who presided at all ceremonies except mass until Holy Innocents' Day (28 December) - was originally confined to cathedrals but spread to smaller churches; and although it was discouraged by the ecclesiastical authorities, whole congregations as well as school boys so delighted in the fun that it was not finally abolished until the reign of Elizabeth I.

One of the few early Acts of Parliament to make reference to schooling for boys and for girls and also to a choice of schools was introduced in 1406. Although in conjunction with legislation relating to labourers and apprentices, the Act included the words "...every man or woman, of what estate or condition that he be, shall be free to set their son or daughter to take learning at any school that pleaseth them within the realm...". How many parents took, or were able to take, advantage of this Statute is debatable; but it does demonstrate that educational opportunity was discussed long before the nineteenth century protagonists became vociferous.

Several of the famous schools in England were founded in the fifteenth century when it became fashionable to establish Song Schools (Sang Schools in Scotland) and Grammar Schools as well as University Colleges. English as a written language was creeping into public documents although Latin remained the official language of formal documentation of Church and State until 1733; even so Chaucer wrote his works in English, Caxton set up his printing press in 1476 to publish English literature in quantity as more of the population became interested in reading, and English Reading Schools were founded. Some schools were adjuncts to chantries while others were established by colleges of Oxford and Cambridge universities, by collegiate churches or by companies and guilds of London and other great cities. Eton College School was founded in 1440 and the City of London School in 1442. For detail on schools in Scotland at this time, see Chapter 13 below. The records of the founding institution, besides those of the school itself, contain useful information on the school, its benefactors and even its early staff appointments and potential pupil market. It should not be forgotten that at this period the university colleges admitted students at the age of 14, later gradually raised to 18; and whereas English was being encouraged in many schools, Oxford and Cambridge, conscious that their graduates were likely to become involved in the documentation of officialdom, insisted on a minimum standard in Latin - an insistence which pertained until the latter half of the present century ! This caused the new Grammar Schools, and even the English Reading Schools, to provide some Latin in their curricula to equip their boys for the new colleges being established at Cambridge (King's in 1441, Queen's in 1448 and St Catherine's in 1473) and at Oxford where Lincoln, All Souls' and Magdalen had been founded by 1458.

The middle of the fifteenth century marked the consolidation of craft guilds which had been growing steadily for 200 years. To encourage and protect the standards of their skills, these guilds had introduced craft apprenticeships, often extremely well organised and demanding high standards. Many Masters, to whom boys and later girls were apprenticed, undertook to provide schooling and education, and in some cases also board and lodging, as well as formal craft training. It would be misleading, however, to conclude that every craftsman was a member of a guild or received formal craft training or even undertook a formal apprenticeship with properly prepared indentures or deeds. Nevertheless, the guilds' records which, particularly for the London-based organisations, have been deposited at the Guildhall Library, London, certainly warrant serious perusal. The librarian there is able to advise what material is available for the London Guilds and Livery Companies.

St Paul's School, London was founded in 1510 by the humanist John Colet, Dean of St Paul's Cathedral, who opened a Grammar School for boys who had completed an elementary education and had demonstrated an aptitude for study. This school was the centre for Humanism in England and helped to transform educational attitudes in many of the old mediaeval schools. By the middle of the sixteenth century about three hundred grammar schools were in existence without being under direct control of the Church. Thus when Henry VIII broke ties with Rome the repercussions on the boys in the English school system were not so severe as in Europe during the religious Reformation there. Those who did suffer were the girls in the British nunneries who received no further schooling for some generations after the closure of those religious houses.

The Chantries Act of 1548 confiscated the estates of the Church expressly to enable the funds so raised to be used in education; however, not all of the money reached scholarly ends in the troubled times for the Church which followed. Nevertheless, during this time many more Public Schools (as the private independent schools are still called in England) were established by Royal Charter and endowed by wealthy merchants and noblemen. Harvests had been good since 1490, trade was expanding and those with businesslike heads were able to take advantage of the improvements. Bedford School was granted letters patent in 1552 by Edward VI and given a large financial sum by Sir William Harper, Lord Mayor of London. The Merchant Taylors' School, a Latin secondary school maintained by the Tailors' Guild in London, was founded in 1561.

The vast majority of these public schools, and very many of the early grammar schools which survived into the present century, have had detailed histories published. They are generally available in the local collections of public libraries in the towns and cities where the schools flourished. Many have produced printed class lists and registers and some include biographical notes on the staff as well as the pupils. Most of these well-established schools have, over the years, published regular journals and magazines of excellent quality containing detailed notes on some of the pupils, recording their sporting and academic achievements, and in many instances reporting on the successes of their former pupils - the "old boys", or in some cases the "old girls". Some of these schools have good libraries of their own and maintain superb records of the many facets of the lives of individuals in their unique scholastic environments. The 'Record of Old Westminsters' and the 'History of Bedford School' are particularly useful.

In sixteenth century Ireland an Act for English Orders, Habits and Language came into force in 1737. This introduced a state system of education to assimilate the Irish to English culture as well as the new Reformed Protestant faith. This concept was reinforced in 1570 by the Dublin Parliament which passed an Act for the Erection of Free Schools; this required a free school to be provided in every diocese and for the schoolmaster to be an Englishman. In Ireland, as in England, the Established Church was determined to stamp out Catholicism and similarly used the schools in furthering this policy.

The Society of Genealogists, 14 Charterhouse Buildings, London EC1M 7BA has an extensive collection and a published catalogue of histories and registers of the well-known public, grammar and endowed schools, and also of many smaller educational institutions within the British Isles.

6. Seventeenth Century School Proposals

As the seventeenth century progressed, several individuals proposed revolutionary ideas in the education field, but at that time England was heading for internal unrest which culminated in the execution of the reigning monarch, Charles I, in 1649; this was followed by a period of Commonwealth Government entirely by Parliament from 1650 until the restoration of the monarchy in 1660. A proposal was made in 1650 by Hartlib and Comenius in their 'London's Charity Enlarged' that a government grant be made for the education of poor children rather than finances be found from Church or private funds. They suggested agricultural schools and state-organised and elementary education. In 1651 Dury published his 'Reformed School' advocating that education be controlled by free educational organisations and not regimented by the State. In keeping with socialistic thinking at that time, of individuals being involved with government of the country and not accepting the dictates of a monarch, he also suggested instruction in the useful arts and sciences rather than in the esoteric classics. John Milton, on the other hand, supported the more traditional education of "our nobler and our gentler youth" rather than becoming involved with "common boys". Milton proposed an academy, to replace the secondary school and the college, in which the ancient classics and also the sciences be taught, yet supported by due subordination to the Bible and Christian teaching.

Little was effected by the State, however, and only philanthropic individuals and organisations became involved with education particularly that of the poor. Several private schools run by women in their own homes for young children were popular in both towns and villages. In these Dame Schools the children were taught the alphabet, reading from the New Testament and were given household chores. The drawing on the cover of this Cameo, based on a painting in the Tate Gallery, London, by Thomas Webster, illustrates how a typical Dame School was conducted. Such private schools, the precursors of nursery or infant schools, lasted well into the nineteenth century, although reports on their organisation and management were often quite disturbing.

Other private schools were organised by women from the early seventeenth century but for a quite different clientele. Particularly around the outskirts of London (at Putney, Hackney and Tottenham, for example) private boarding schools were established for girls of good family from all over England. Reading in Latin, Greek, Italian and French, as well as writing, music, dancing and household skills were taught by resident and visiting teachers. Girls, whose scholastic needs had been virtually disregarded since the closure of the nunneries, once more had educational opportunities. The records, where extant, of such academies can be found in local collections.

The ideals of Hartlib, Comenius and Dury came to abrupt end with the restoration of the monarchy in 1660; furthermore, the established Church of England with its organisation, which included administering Church Schools, was refounded on even firmer footings. The 1662 Act of Uniformity required all schoolmasters and tutors to be loyal to the Church of England and confirmed the 1603 Canon for them to be licensed by the bishop on pain of imprisonment or fine. The Bishops' Subscription Books, today in county record offices, are interesting research sources, particularly as they contain the qualifications and signatures of the teachers themselves. The 1665 Five Mile Act not only made it illegal for a nonconformist minister to come within five miles of a corporate town, but forbade any nonconformist to teach in a public or private school. Separate Dissenting Schools were thus founded, albeit illegally, and to avoid too great a conflict with "the establishment" dissenters concentrated on teaching practical subjects and their number increased considerably following the Toleration Act of 1689. Daniel Defoe, Isaac Watts and Samuel Wesley were later products of such schools. However, a trend had been created for Anglicans to follow a classical academic education and for nonconformists to turn towards industrial training - a pattern which persisted for generations. Dissenting Academies, which also leaned away from the arts, appeared around the country after the Toleration Act - the one in Northamptonshire at Daventry, for example, producing the famous scientist Joseph Priestley. In Ireland Catholic masters taught in barns and even in hedgerows to avoid detection; hence the so-called Hedge Schools, often termed Pay Schools as the parents were prepared to pay for Catholic education.

7. Charity, Voluntary and Military Schools

Towards the end of the seventeenth century Charity Schools were developed to educate and clothe the children of the poor, free of charge. It was felt that the provision of education would alleviate poverty and thus such schools appeared in the poorer urban centres, rather than in rural areas. Some Charity Schools were specifically for city orphans and so provided boarding facilities or hospitality and were often termed "hospitals". At Christ's Hospital in London and Hertford, a typical example, they even called the boarding houses "wards" with initially about 25 boys in each being catered and cared for by a "nurse". By the nineteenth century the boys all ate in a common dining hall and one nurse had responsibility for up to 70 boys. On the London campus there were about 600 boys aged from 9 to 19 and at Hertford 400 boys aged from 7 to 11 but with only four teaching staff: a writing master (who also acted as school steward) with two ushers as assistants and one grammar master. It is evident that in the grammar school the one master had to rely heavily on the more advanced pupils to help in teaching the junior boys; even in the writing school the master and his two assistants used senior boys to instruct the juniors. However, it is encouraging to note that those who remained at the school from 16 to 19 were preparing to go to university, so dispelling the myth that sons of only wealthy families attained that level. Most charity schools were similarly organised. Also known as Blue Coat, Green Coat or Grey Coat Schools, after the uniforms worn by their pupils, they were supported by private contributions but often operated by a religious body. For example, the SPCK (see Chapter 3 above) became involved from 1698 with setting up Charity Schools to provide full-time education for children of the deserving poor - in fact there was little alternative education for poor children throughout the eighteenth century. For teachers as well, Charity Schools were attractive - they provided an annual salary whereas in other schools there was little guarantee of a known income. The deep religious influence can be seen from the instructions given to the parents when their children were admitted to the SPCK Charity Schools :

ORDERS
TO BE READ AND GIVEN TO THE PARENTS,
ON THE
ADMITTANCE OF THEIR CHILDREN
TO THE CHARITY-SCHOOLS;
AND TO BE SET UP IN THEIR HOUSES.

1.That the parents take care to send their children to school at the school hour, and keep them at home on no pretence whatsoever, except in case of sickness.

2.That they send their children clean washed and combed.

3.That in regard the trustees of this school will take due care that the children shall suffer no injuries by their master or mistress's correction, which is only designed for their good: the parents shall freely submit their children to undergo the discipline of the school, when guilty of any faults, and forbear coming thither on such occasions: so that the children may not be countenanced in their faults, nor the master or mistress discouraged in the performance of their duty.

4.That it is the duty of parents to keep their children in good order when they are at home, by good example and admonition.

5.That they teach their children at home their catechism, and read the Holy Scriptures, especially on the Lord's Day, and use prayers morning and evening in their families; so that both parents and children may be better informed of their duty, and by a constant and sincere practice thereof procure the blessing of God upon them.

6.That the children attend at the Parish Church on the Lord's Day (commonly called Sunday), both in the morning and afternoon, and holidays, Wednesdays and Fridays; and that the master and mistress respectively take notice of their behaviour, and of those who shall be absent at any of those times.

7.That the parents do not take their children out of school, without first obtaining leave of the trustees; and whatever child shall be so removed without leave, before that time, shall not have clothes or books, nor any other child of those parents taken into the schools.

8.If the parents do not observe the said orders, their children are to be dismissed the school, and to forfeit their school clothes.

Ye fathers provoke not your children to wrath, but bring them up in the nurture and admonition of the Lord: having them in subjection with all gravity. Eph.vi.4., 1 Tim.iii.4.

Honour thy father and thy mother that it may be well with thee, and thou mayest live long on the earth. Eph.vi.2-3.

It has been asserted that Cromwell's Parliamentary generals were the founders of army education; their issuing in 1643 of the 'Soldier's Pocket Bible' and in 1644 of 'The Soldier's Catechism' with the recommendation that all ranks "read and observe what hath been written by eminent soldiers" is quoted in support for this assertion. One could even claim that State involvement in education began at this point. It is thought that the issue of the Bibles and Catechisms produced a remarkable increase of literacy amongst the non-commissioned Parliamentarians; however, the first reference to a military school is a request in 1662 for a schoolmaster by the officers at Fort St George, Madras to the East India Company. In 1685 the Tangier garrison possessed three schoolmasters: one a graduate, one a clerk and schoolmaster, and one an usher, writing master and gunner.

Within the English navy, education officers were appointed towards the end of the seventeenth century; their duties were to instruct ships' young officers in reading, writing, arithmetic and navigation and also to teach other young people associated in any way with the ship. The Naval Academy was founded at Portsmouth in 1729 and reorganised in 1806 as the Royal Naval College. This was closed in 1837 but re-opened in 1838 under the same name as a training college for serving officers. In 1873 it moved to Greenwich - the location mentioned in the Preface. A visitation by Admiralty officials in 1749 to the Academy, while still effectively a school at Portsmouth, prompted the following account to appear in the minutes of the Admiralty's Secretary's Department: "There they awarded 5gns to a pupil who was specially recommended as 'a most Ingenious deserving lad'". They also discussed with the Headmaster whether the pupils should be taught Latin, but concurred with his opinion "it would interfere with and be Prejudicial to their other Studies, more essentially necessary in the Profession for which they were designed"; a petition by the "Young Gentlemen" that "the Old Yacht" lying in the harbour might be utilised for their practical instruction in sailing, was granted. However, the standards of these early naval attempts at education were poor and continued to be so for well over 100 years until after the report of the Newcastle Commission in 1861.

Workhouse Schools were attached to the parish workhouses, particularly after the General Workhouse Act of 1723 when the Overseers of the Poor could engage a schoolmaster. The emphasis, however, was more on practical subjects, to enable the pupils to be subsequently apprenticed and thereby no longer a burden on the parish. Records of such schools are to be found in parish documents or in archives of the Guardians of the Poor in county record offices, as are any surviving subsequent apprenticeship records for the successful pupils.

In about 1730 Circulating Schools were founded by Rev Griffith Jones in Wales as English Charity Schools were not proving a success there, even though Welsh Bibles had been issued in them. The principle behind the Welsh Charity Schools was for a parish to support one school initially and then, as funds became available, to support a second. The SPCK also provided funds such that within seven years there were 37 flourishing Circulating Schools. Before Jones died in 1761 there were 218 of these schools in Wales in which 10,000 persons had been taught in one year to read the Scriptures in their native tongue; and between 1737 and 1760 150,212 persons had been instructed in reading the Welsh Bible. However, not all the pupils were children, as the First Report of the Society for the Support of the Gaelic Schools in the Highlands and Islands of Scotland makes clear : "At these Circulating Schools, so anxious were the people to learn their own native language, that persons of all ages attended, from six years of age to above seventy. In several places, indeed, the older people formed about two-thirds of the number in attendance. Persons above sixty, attended every day; and often lamented, nay even wept, that they had not learned forty or fifty years sooner. Not infrequently the children actually taught their parents; and sometimes the parents and children of one family resorted to the same Circulating School, during its short continuance in a district; while various individuals, who, from great age, were obliged to wear spectacles, seized the opportunity, and learned to read the Scriptures in Welsh, at that advanced period of life".

In Scotland there was increasing dissatisfaction with the schools concentrating on a classical curriculum and so the practical ideas of Comenius of a century earlier (see Chapter 6 above) were revived. In 1746 at Ayr Grammar School for example, navigation and surveying with arithmetic and geometry were introduced to prepare the pupils "for business in the most expeditious and effectual way possible", while science was taught in Perth from 1761. These institutions were not charity or voluntary schools in the accepted sense, but the town councils which ran them (see Chapter 13 below)did provide free tuition for those pupils whose parents could not afford to pay.

There is evidence of Adult Schools being proposed in the eighteenth century and some were formally established: John Pierson and John Reynolds taught adults to read in 1700 under the auspices of the SPCK - which in 1711 recommended adult evening classes. From 1789 the Birmingham Sunday Society catered for those who had outgrown the Sunday Schools; from 1798 an Adult School was opened in Nottingham by William Singleton and Samuel Fox, respectively a Methodist and a Quaker.

However, if the family or social historian or the genealogist can find no reference to the schooling of his ancestors in the mid- eighteenth century, this is easily understandable. The infant mortality rate was amazingly high - in London, for example, it has been suggested that 75% of even the baptised children died before attaining the age of five - and so to send one's child to school was a dubious investment. More significantly, for the average labourer there was little call for education: he worked long hours with no spare time to read, and reading material was expensive anyway; if he could write he had no one to write to - everybody he knew lived in the parish, or a nearby one, and if he had anything to communicate he walked there and said it. It was only when the population became more mobile, with the advent of better roads and the new canals towards the end of the century, that craftsmen and tradesmen had to begin to keep sensible accounts and thus required a knowledge of reading, writing and arithmetic. In Ireland the lack of refer- ences stems from a different cause. Schooling for Catholics was being provided in the prolific Hedge or Pay Schools, but illegally. It was reported to the Dublin House of Lords in 1731 that there were 552 known Hedge Schools in the country. But because they should not have been operating (Catholics were not permitted to teach from 1691 to 1782), the usual types of schools records are almost non-existent - even though their educational success was an enigmatic headache for the authorities.

Meanwhile for those in military service there was greater hope. The Royal Military Academy was founded at Woolwich in 1741 for cadets and for the professional education of all "the raw and inexperienced people belonging to the military branch of the Ordnance"; both theoretical and practical subjects were offered but in two distinct schools within the Academy. In the theoretical school pure and mixed mathematics were taught while in the practical school the various gun drills etc. were taught. Discipline was strict for the apparently boisterous cadets: any found swimming in the Thames were to be taken out and carried naked to the guard-room - but, as can be clearly seen in the records, still the young men defied the rules and regulations. Besides cadets the Academy was attended in the early days by supernumeraries who were permitted to study the three Rs pending vacancies. Moreover, certain students, also known as "gentlemen attendants" who did not intend joining the army, were permitted to avail themselves of the tuition by paying an annual fee of thirty guineas. Even classics as well as mathematics were taught at the schools in the Warren, not within the campus of the artillery and engineers, but attached to the Academy at the foot of Shooters Hill, Woolwich.

The first reference within the army to a unit school is that of the Grenadier Guards in 1762 when they were at the Tower of London. The Royal Hibernian Military School in Dublin grew out of the Hibernian Society which had been "maintaining, educating and apprenticing the orphans and children of soldiers only", according to an account in the preface to the first edition (1767) of 'Military Medley' by Thomas Simes, a Captain of the Queens Royal Regiment of Foot. At a meeting of the governors and guardians at Dublin Castle on 27 May 1765 it was reported by Samuel Burrows the secretary, that originally ten boys, and then a further ten had been cared for by private benefaction in what really amounted to a military charity school; a subscription raised in March 1765 enabled another 20 boys to be provided for but there were 1500 "in the utmost indigence" about a half of whom were orphans. The main concern, however, seemed to be to ensure the children were taught the Protestant faith and "not only to rescue unfortunate children from perdition, but to rear them up in a due sense of religion and industry and to give them such trades and occupations as may render their hands of real use to the public". It was hoped that "as soon as a proper fund will permit, to enlarge and extend this plan as much to the care of the daughters as the sons of soldiers". The school thrived until vacating its premises in 1922.

In the army Regulations and Orders "very proper to be given by the Colonel of a Regiment of Foot" published in 1767 in Simes' 'Medley' referred to above, the education of soldiers and their children is clearly considered: "A serjeant or corporal whose sobriety, honesty and good conduct can be depended upon; and who is capable of teaching writing, reading and arithmetic is to be employed to act in the capacity of a school-master, by whom soldiers and soldiers' children are to be carefully instructed. A room is to be appointed for that use, and it would be highly commendable if the Chaplain, or his deputy, would pay attention to the conduct of the school". Further reference to education is given later in the 'Medley': "When the Regiment is ordered into cantonments....the serjeant or corporal appointed to act as School-master....are to be kept at headquarters". The 9th Foot also appointed a sergeant to teach backward recruits; an inspecting general complimented the 80th Foot on a school for the soldiers' children. The Royal Artillery opened a regimental school in 1797 with a sergeant, named Dougherty, as schoolmaster.

The school of the Royal Scots was so efficient that the magistrates of Stirling requested that local people "might participate in its benefits". The Duke of York's School at Chelsea for the maintenance, support and education of regular soldiers' children was opened in 1801. When the Rifle Brigade was formed in 1802, instruction in reading, writing and arithmetic were components of normal training. The Royal Military College was founded at Sandhurst in 1812 to ensure that officers received a formal education. Within the armed services, education for the children of serving men and officers continued in the nineteenth and twentieth centuries, often ahead of their counterparts in civilian life. The daughters of soldiers, for example, received tuition after 1840 when schoolmistresses were appointed for this purpose to every regiment or regimental depot. The daughters of naval officers were similarly accommodated, as described in Chapter 8 below. Regimental archivists and published regimental histories should be consulted on the records available for army educational establishments and similarly the admiralty should be contacted for details on naval schools. The War Office Library may be able to assist with information on military education.

In eighteenth century civilian England, Sunday Schools were introduced from 1780 by Robert Raikes the publisher and editor of the Gloucester Journal, basing his ideas on those of Rev Thomas Stock who had already run a Sunday School in Gloucester; these became so popular that by 1785 the Society for the Establishment and Support of Sunday Schools was formed to co-ordinate their activities. Its aims were to "encourage industry and virtue, dispel the darkness of ignorance, diffuse the light of knowledge [and] bring men cheerfully to submit to their station". Even in the previous year John Wesley had observed in his journal "I find these schools springing up wherever I go". Queen Charlotte added her support in 1787. In fact by 1895 the Society had distributed 91,915 spelling books, 24,232 Testaments and 5,360 Bibles. An inter-denominational Sunday School Union was formed in 1803 which further strengthened the work of the Sunday Schools. Their curricula comprised mostly Bible Reading lessons, but at least reading was encouraged. Some factory owners opened Sunday Schools at their works where reading and writing were taught. The monitorial system used at Winchester School a century and more before was revived by Bell and Lancaster to overcome the severe shortage of teachers. A professional teacher addressed up to 1000 children seated in rows with a monitor in each row. The monitors then passed on the skills of reading, writing, arithmetic, spelling or the higher subjects mostly by rote learning. Discipline was maintained at some of the Sunday Schools for children by a Beadle or "Nobbler", who in his uniform at a number of schools also had ceremonial duties such as leading an annual procession of all the pupils through the local town. Some Sunday Schools expanded rapidly: Stockport, Cheshire with over 5000 pupils was said to be the largest in the world. During the 1790s the Sunday Schools broadened their influence by including anthologies of stories, songs and poetry in their teaching material; the Methodists, for example, opened their own Sunday Schools in Bristol in 1804 - which by 1814 were affording education to 2248 boys and girls. Jewish schools were founded while other denominations established similar Dissenters' Academies to provide educa-tion for their followers' children.

The Freemasons established the Royal Masonic Institution for Girls in 1788 and the Royal Masonic Institution for Boys in 1798. Known colloquially as Masonic Schools, both were charitable institutions providing education for the children of members of masonic lodges throughout the British Isles. Although records from the mid-nineteenth century have survived, being of private bodies they are not available for public research.

No longer could the government stand aside and watch a multitudinous variety of commercial and charitable, established and dissenting, individuals and organisations attempt to educate rich or poor. And so at long last Parliament was motivated and in 1802 an Act was passed regulating the working conditions of apprentices which required, inter alia, that male and female apprentices be provided with free part-time education. Among the conditions of this Act the influence of the Church was most evident:

VI...That every such Apprentice shall be instructed, in some Part of every working Day, for the First Four Years at least of his or her Apprenticeship...in the usual hours of work, in Reading, Writing and Arithmetick...by some discreet and proper Person, to be provided and paid for by the Master or Mistress of such Apprentice...

VII...That the Room or Apartment in which any Male Apprentice shall sleep, shall be entirely separate and distinct from the Room or Apartment in which any Female Apprentice shall sleep; and that not more than Two Apprentices shall in any Case sleep in the same Bed...

VIII...That every Apprentice shall for the Space of One Hour at least every Sunday, be instructed and examined in the Principles of the Christian Religion...

However, a Bill introduced in 1807 by Whitbread to provide two years' free education for every child, financed from the poor rate, was thrown out by the House of Lords. Factory Schools, such as those founded by cotton-mill owner Robert Owen, were based on the principle that the best work can be obtained only from happy, prosperous and well-educated employees. Although the project financed by Owen himself floundered, his principles were embraced by others and Factory and Colliery Schools were established in particular areas. Owen had inspired his peers to set up infant schools and in 1818 he provided the teacher for the first Infant School to be opened in London. The second was opened in 1820 at Spitalfields with Samuel Wilderspin as the teacher. In 1824 the Infant School Society was created by Wilderspin to expand the concept and within a year there were 25 throughout England.

The growth of voluntary societies, therefore, continued with the establishment in 1808 of the Royal Lancastrian Institution (named after Joseph Lancaster, a Quaker and the monitorial system advocate) (but called the British and Foreign School Society from 1814) and in 1811 of the National Society for Promoting the Education of the Poor in the Principles of the Established Church (based on similar ideas of Andrew Bell, a Scot and an Anglican clergyman). Bell had published his method in 1797 in 'An Experiment in Education' based on his experiences of teaching soldiers' orphans in Madras with very little support from local teachers. Lancaster had published a similar but more precise method in 1803 in his 'Improvements in Education' as a means of instructing very many children with only one teacher. The Royal Lancastrian Institution was formed to promote "the Education of the Labouring and Manufacturing Classes of Society of every Religious Persuasion"; thus nonconformists tended to send their children to these schools, in preference to the National Schools. However, the National Society financed by the Anglican Church of England with its nationwide parish organisation rapidly became the most influential educational body in the country. Even so the quality of teaching left much to be desired and not every child attended these schools. The teaching in the British Society's Schools soon became markedly evangelical and so Unitarians, Jews and Roman Catholics were opposed to sending their children to these schools which were most definitely not non-sectarian.

Ragged Schools were established by philanthropists such as Cranfield in South London (1810), and Pounds at Portsmouth, to provide free education for poor children. The Field Lane Refuge in London was opened in 1843 and the following year the Ragged School Union was founded with support from Lord Shaftesbury to co-ordinate the several charitable bodies for the care, as well as the education, of the destitute poor and outcast children in particular. The annual reports on individual schools illustrate the pathetic conditions of the children and their lives at home. In some cases the schools helped the children to provide for themselves and their families; in Sheffield, for example, the ragged school at Peacroft organised and publicised in the local paper a Shoeblack Brigade in 1856 for boys to clean shoes in the streets or in homes by appointment. The boys wore a red badge displaying the school name to prove their authenticity and they were given police protection. A proportion of their earnings was invested in a Savings Bank on their behalf, a proportion in materials, and although each boy retained half for his immediate use, separate Bread and Clothing Funds were also established by the school. Extra night classes were organised for those pupils who were working as shoeblacks during the day. Day and Evening Schools (the term specifically given to evening classes established at this period for providing elementary education to illiterate adults) and also Sunday Schools were established across the country by the Ragged School Union, which in 1914 changed its name to the Shaftesbury Society and Ragged School Union.

Dr George Birkbeck and Lord (Henry) Brougham were instrumental in founding evening classes in the form of Mechanics' Institutes from 1823. Within thirty years some 610 of these were providing theoretical continuation instruction in mathematics and science to support the practical tasks in the workshops and factories being undertaken by over half a million students. Unfortunately there was too large a gap in the standards between the Mechanics Institutes and the pupils' former elementary schooling, and coupled with the lack of suitable instructors there were many withdrawals. Other philanthropic individuals and organisations provided evening classes and private Night Schools were founded; but it was not until government funding became available from 1851 that this further education became more successful.

Adult Schools, organised and supported mainly by the Quakers, gathered popularity from 1811. These schools usually met early on a Sunday morning, or on a Sunday evening for reading and writing lessons, followed by Bible instruction and discussions. As they developed over the years libraries, savings banks, and sick benefits were made available to members. Such schools were still flourishing in England after the First World War and had spread, under their National Council, to Canada, the United States of America, Africa, Australia and New Zealand. Although one of the earliest schools in Britain exclusively for the instruction of adults was opened in Bala, North Wales in the summer of 1811, adults had been able to receive some education in Wales from 1730 at least, as described above. There was also a Welsh Charity School in Monmouth in 1754 at which it was noted "there was an old man, seventy-one years of age, with five other people far advanced in years, who came there with their little children to be taught to read the Word of God". The Episcopal Minister in Bala, Thomas Chambers, commented in 1811 "What involved me first to think of establishing such an Institution, was the adversion I found in the adults to associate with the children in their schools" - although the commentaries of 1730 and 1760 do not seem to bear this out.

On 8 March 1812 the first Adult Schools in Bristol were opened due to the exertions of William Smith, a doorkeeper of a local Methodist Chapel, who was involved with the Bristol Auxiliary Bible Society - linked to the British and Foreign Bible Society which had been founded in 1804. Smith was initially helping to raise funds to provide the poor of Bristol with bibles, but he realised they could not read. He persuaded those with means, particularly Stephen Prust, to loan him two rooms, to loan him bibles and other books and secure the services of former Charity School teachers - and so he was able to offer teaching in one room for men and in the second room for women. Within a few weeks Thomas Martin, a Methodist minister in Bristol formed "An Institution for Instructing Adult Persons to Read the Holy Scriptures" which was funded by subscriptions. From this emerged the Bristol Society for Promoting the Education of Adults to which several influential Quakers were drawn, who in turn provided accommodation for further adult schooling. By the beginning of 1814 there were 22 schools for men and 24 for women in and around Bristol.

Adult Schools were founded elsewhere in England within a few years - Plymouth and Bath in 1813, Southwark in March 1814, High Wycombe in September 1814, for which the Prince Regent was Patron, the City of London in July 1815, and then around the world following the publication in 1814 of the first edition of Dr Thomas Pole's 'History of the Origin and Progress of Adult Schools'. There appears to have been infinite opportunity for the adults - a report from Manchester referred to a poor woman of 98 daily attending a boys' school "to receive instruction from one of the Monitors; and she reads in an audible manner to the school" - and at Glencalvie a man of 107 who had enlisted in the school in 1715 and attended frequently, was still attempting to learn to read in 1815, but his learning was hampered by his failing sight.

Another type of Adult School was opened in Bristol "for the instruction of those poor unhappy young women who have swerved from the paths of virtue, and who, from a consciousness of having fallen into a state of moral degradation, were ashamed to go to the other schools; or whose company would not be acceptable amongst even the poor of superior character".

8. Government Involvement in Education

A state-subsidised non-sectarian national education system, although desirable, could not be introduced in England because of sectarian rivalries; and yet in 1831, as amplified in Chapter 14 below, the government was able to implement such a system in Ireland. The pressure increased on the voluntary societies to provide a wider education and in 1839 the British and Foreign School Society published its first secular reader as a companion text to scripture lessons. In the meantime the government had paid (annually since 1833) grants, initially of £20,000 to the British and to the National Society Schools; by 1850 the grants were £200,000 to all denominational schools. This development in policy was due to political emancipation being achieved by nonconformists and Roman Catholics by 1829 and through the Reform Act of 1832. All religious groups had, therefore, a right to be treated equally and the thousand or so schools supported by all nonconformists, Roman Catholics and Jews which were either founded, or more firmly established, were entitled to financial aid from the State. By 1858 government expenditure on education in England and Wales had become £700,000 and by 1861 over £800,000 per year.

Because the government was investing money in children's education, a Committee of the Privy Council was set up to consider "all matters affecting the education of the people". Its first secretary was Dr James Kay-Shuttleworth a former Manchester doctor who had become one of the Assistant Commissioners in London for the New Poor Law. Schools inspectors were appointed to report to the Committee of Privy Council on Education (which became the Education Department in 1856) on, inter alia, the nature and method of instruction. The question of who should be consulted when inspectors were being considered for appointment in the variety of schools having loyalties to polarised doctrinal beliefs was never really resolved. The Church of England, for example, insisted that Inspectors' Reports should be sent to the appropriate Bishop and Archbishop, whereas the Wesleyans made no comparable stipulations. The Committee also introduced the concepts of teacher training and pupil teachers.

The comprehensive surveys in 1851 of English, Welsh and Scottish educational facilities illustrated that nearly all children were able to receive at least some day-schooling through the combined efforts of Church and State, although mostly at Anglican Church Schools. The 1851 Education Census of England and Wales is packed with fascinating details and the appendix brims over with statistics on counties and even some registration districts or poor law unions. For example, Table T shows that in Northampton Borough there were 1818 males and 1610 females attending 58 Day Schools of which 45 were privately funded, and in 27 Sunday Schools there were 2131 males and 2169 females; and this was from a total population of 13,335 males and 13,322 females, a balance between the sexes hardly equalled anywhere else in the country. The occupations of Adult Evening School scholars were analysed in Table W: Northamptonshire had a total of 329 adults of whom there were 83 agricultural labourers, 16 lacemakers (the only ones for the entire country), 24 artizans and 206 with no stated occupations. This compares with 652 adults in Bedfordshire of whom there were 7 domestic servants, 340 agricultural labourers, 122 artizans and 183 having no stated occupations. In Monmouth from a total of 170, there was 1 chemist, 21 domestic servants, 16 agricultural labourers, 25 miners, 56 artizans and 41 whose occupation was not stated. In the 'Tables of Occupations of Young Persons under 15 Years of Age', where the figures are broken into those under 5, from 5 to 10 and from 10 to 15, there were 36 males occupied in vermin destroying, 90 males in publishing and bookselling (and that was long before Lochin Publishing had been established to produce these Cameos); but most astoundingly there were 282 male and 405 female school teachers - obviously involved as pupil-teachers or in the monitorial systems of Bell or Lancaster. Whilst the 1851 Education Census for Scotland was organised slightly differently, its results merit perusal. The reader is encouraged to study the returns for those areas of England and Wales of immediate interest published as Parliamentary Papers (1852-3, xc) and (1852-3, lxxix), and reprinted in 1854, when the Scottish material (1854,lix) though less well analysed was published.

In 1851 the government, realising the value of further education which until this time was being provided mostly from the private sector, made additional

CLASSIFICATION OF DAY SCHOOLS.

(according to their Sources of Maintenance.)

SUMMARY OF ENGLAND AND WALES.

DESCRIPTION OF SCHOOLS.	No. of Schools*	Number of Scholars belonging to the Schools.†			DESCRIPTION OF SCHOOLS.	No. of Schools.	Number of Scholars belonging to the Schools.		
		Both Sexes.	M.	F.			Both Sexes.	M.	F.
ALL DAY SCHOOLS	44,836	2,108,592	1,139,324	969,268	CLASS III.—*cont.* *Denominational—cont.*				
					Moravians - - -	7	366	218	148
PUBLIC DAY SCHOOLS -	15,411	1,413,170	795,632	617,538	Wesleyan Methodists— *British*	20	3,082	1,805	1,277
PRIVATE DAY SCHOOLS -	29,425	695,422	343,692	351,730	" *Others*	343	36,582	22,535	14,047
					Methodist New Con- nexion— *British*	3	667	430	217
Classification of Public Schools.					" *Others*	10	1,148	618	530
CLASS I.—SUPPORTED BY GENERAL OR LOCAL TAXATION - - -	610	48,826	28,708	20,118	Primitive Methodists— *British*	2	206	103	103
					" *Others*	23	1091	520	571
CLASS II.—SUPPORTED BY ENDOWMENTS - -	3,125	206,279	138,495	67,784	Bible Christians— *British*	1	64	26	38
					" *Others*	7	303	171	132
CLASS III. — SUPPORTED BY RELIGIOUS BODIES -	10,595	1,048,851	509,300	479,551	Wesleyan Methodist Association	10	1,112	616	496
					Calvinistic Methodists— *British*	22	1,759	1,085	674
CLASS IV.—OTHER PUB- LIC SCHOOLS -	1,081	109,214	59,129	50,085	" *Others*	19	1,055	599	456
					Lady Huntingdon's Con- nexion - *British*	1	80	..	80
CLASS I.					" *Others*	8	504	306	258
Military Schools - -	33	3,348	2,560	788	New Church - -	9	1,551	891	660
Naval Schools - -	14	2,348	1,963	385	Dissenters (not defined) — *British*	28	3,851	2,398	1,453
Woods and Forests School	1	259	135	124	*Others*	15	1,541	861	680
Corporation Schools - -	3	2,394	1,364	1,030	Lutherans - - -	1	157	107	50
Workhouse Schools - -	523	38,067	20,660	17,407	French Protestants -	1	15	..	15
Prison Schools - - -	34	2,410	2,126	384	German Missionary Society - - -	1	100	40	60
					Isolated Congrega- tions— *British*	2	184	130	54
CLASS II.						12	960	479	481
Collegiate and Grammar Schools - - -	586	35,612	32,221	3,391	Roman Catholics - -	311	38,583	20,501	18,082
Other Endowed Schools ‡ -	2,559	170,667	106,274	64,393	Jews - - - -	10	1,234	735	499
					Undenominational.				
CLASS III.					British - - -	814	82,597	52,037	30,560
Denominational.					Others - - -	4	1,063	553	510
Ch. of England— *National*	3,730	464,975	253,934	211,041					
" *British*	12	1,043	600	443	**CLASS IV.**				
" *Others*	4,839	335,489	169,206	166,283	Ragged Schools (*exclusive of those supported by religious bodies*) §	123	22,337	12,705	9,632
Ch. of Scotland— *British*	1	130	130	..	Orphan Schools - -	39	3,764	1,712	2,052
" *Others*	4	816	522	294	Blind Schools - -	11	609	342	267
United Presbyterians -	3	217	148	69	Deaf and Dumb Schools	9	392	212	190
Presbyterian Church in England— *British*	2	96	48	48	School for Idiots -	1	18	16	2
" *Others*	23	2,361	1,561	800	Factory Schools - -	115	17,834	9,724	8,110
Scottish Presbyterians	1	345	195	150	Colliery Schools - -	41	3,511	2,013	1,498
Presbyterians (not otherwise defined)— *British*	1	263	143	120	Chemical Works Schools	4	832	433	399
" *Others*	6	1,058	607	451	Foundry School - -	1	103	55	48
Independents —*British*	183	22,596	12,586	10,012	Mechanics' Institution Schools - - -	5	1,564	1,223	341
" *Others*	246	34,806	13,833	10,975	Industrial Schools -	6	607	383	224
Baptists— *British*	51	4,946	2,895	2,051	Agricultural Schools	3	284	213	61
" *Others*	64	3,719	1,861	1,858	Railway Schools - -	5	843	440	412
Society of Friends— *British*	5	577	247	330	Philanthropic Society's Farm School - -	1	96	96	..
" *Others*	13	1,670	990	680	Other Subscription Schools of no specific character -	717	56,441	29,582	26,859
Unitarians— *British*	4	882	649	233					
" *Others*	26	2,854	1,322	1,532	Total of British Schools of all Descriptions -	852	123,015	75,332	47,683

* By the term "school" is here meant a distinct establishment; thus, a school for boys and girls, if under one general management and conducted in one range of building is regarded as only one school, although the tuition may be carried on in separate compartments of the building, under separate superintendence.

† It has not been thought necessary to encumber these Tables with the number of scholars attending each class of day schools. The total number attending all private schools and the aggregate of public schools is given in the previous summary (Table A.); and there is nothing to lead to the conclusion that the proportion of attendance is materially greater in one class of public schools than in another. See the facts given respecting two counties; post, page cxxxviii.

‡ For a minuter classification of these schools, see Supplement I. to Table B., page cxxiv.

§ The total number of Ragged Schools is 132, containing 22,543 scholars.

1851 Education Census - Table B

grants to elementary day schools which provided continuation classes. The popularity of these classes increased until the 1876 Education Act made elementary education compulsory anyway. From 1893 adults were permitted to join the evening classes in elementary education and total attendances increased once more.

Voluntary reformatories such as the Philanthropic Society's school at Redhill in Surrey and Captain Brenton's Asylum at Hackney in London (Middlesex) had been established early in the nineteenth century; but the growth of juvenile delinquency had been so enormous in the 1840s that a Select Committee of the House of Lords was set up which resulted in two Youth Offenders Acts in 1854. While the Select Committee was still sitting further Reformatory Schools were founded by local effort or by private enterprise but the 1854 Acts required the Home Office to certify residential Reformatory Schools (which became known also as Certified Industrial Schools) to which boys and girls under the age of 16 who had served at least fourteen days in gaol could be transferred. The number of permitted pupils at each school was stated at the time of its certification. There were also uncertified Industrial Schools, normally residential, at which children who suffered from neglect or who had come from destitute homes might attend. Both types of school taught the children, besides basic education, a trade with the intention of introducing them into society as useful citizens after their period at school. There were, in addition, several Reformatory Ship Schools certified from the late 1850s although some of them became shore-based during the present century. A number of these ships suffered arson attacks from the pupils who were rehoused in similar or in shore-based reformatories.

The Industrial Schools Act of 1857 empowered magistrates to commit certain young offenders whose life-style was considered likely to lead to criminality directly to the Industrial Schools. Further Acts in 1860 and 1861 reinforced this concept although the schools were known by a variety of titles: Truant Schools (which became Short Term or Industrial Schools), Special Schools (for mentally and physically handicapped children such as an 'Industrial School for the Blind' which was established in Sheffield in 1860), Day Industrial Schools, Training Schools, Farm Schools and Schools of Discipline. In 1866 another Industrial Schools Act enabled local authorities to grant financial aid from local rates to residential denominational Industrial Schools - these were beginning to be established for young offenders whose parents were not within the Anglican Church. However, it was not until 1890 that any of the Reformatory Schools became substitutes for prison sentences for the young. The Day Industrial Schools referred to above were instituted in 1876 to deal with young persons whose parents refused to send them to school following the 1870 Education Act; in general, however, these Day Schools were a failure - the parents having a greater influence than the magistrates' power - and such schools mostly closed before the First World War. The remaining Reformatory and Industrial Schools became Approved Schools in 1933. The Annual Reports of the Inspector of Reformatory Schools from No 1 in 1857 to No 59 in 1915, which are available in microform, provide interesting detail on this type of school (the later reports are of the Inspector of Reformatory and Industrial Schools). The report of the Royal (Lord Aberdare) Commission on the conditions of Certified Reformatory and Industrial Schools, published in 1884 in two parts (PP.1884,xlv), includes the type of education provided in these institutions. The detailed evidence in the second part is most illuminating. The educational standards in these institutions are detailed in greater depth in the report of another (the Lushington) enquiry (PP.1896, c.8204,xlv). In general the records of such schools are retained by them or have been deposited in the local county archives. These Industrial Schools or Reformatory Schools should not be confused with those institutions, also called Industrial Schools, which were supported by and attached to industry for the purpose of providing law-abiding, but frequently poor, children with an education geared to the requirements of that industry.

The cost to the Government of education in 1858 caused a Royal (the Newcastle) Commission on Popular Education to be set up to report its findings in 1861. To economise, the grant system was abolished and payment by results was introduced whereby schools were paid four shillings for every child in attendance and two shillings and eight pence per subject for every child who passed an annual examination in reading, writing and arithmetic. Detailed instructions were given in the Commission's Report on conducting and marking the examinations. A further economy was effected by withdrawing government grants towards the cost of building teacher-training colleges. The well- established colleges, particularly those of the Church of England Schools, were thus unaffected; but the newer groups, having been able to legally join the education field only since 1830, became left even further behind.

The Newcastle Commission also reported on the conditions in the Navy Schools which, as stated above, had never been particularly good. Attendance records were badly kept and the teaching standards were low. It was felt that the Captains and Senior Officers were to blame and one reason for schoolmasters being inferior was the poor wages being offered. Following these findings, and similar situations being discovered in the Dockyards Schools, conditions were greatly improved over the ensuing years. There were, however, two exceptions to the inferior standards found within the naval educational system. In 1830 a Royal Naval School had been founded for the sons of Naval and Marine Officers, and ten years later their sisters were similarly provided for: the Royal Naval Female School was founded at Richmond on 2 April 1840 "to bestow upon the daughters of necessitous Naval and Marine Officers, of and above ward-room rank at the lowest reduction of cost practicable, a good virtuous and religious education, in conformity with the principles and doctrines of the Church of England". Thus although this girls' school could have been the vanguard of a totally new concept, being established within the armed forces and after the religious emancipation and Reform Acts of the previous decade, the founders chose to tie its charter to the Established Church in preference to creating a non-sectarian system.

The Clarendon Commission in 1861 recognised only nine Public Schools in England; these were so named because they offered education to boys (and later to girls) of the general public from all over the country, in contradistinction to the Church and voluntary schools which normally catered for children from a specific area. Winchester, Eton, Westminster, St Paul's and Merchant Taylors' had their origins in centuries past although Charterhouse, Harrow, Rugby and Shrewsbury offered similar facilities. Another Royal Commission, the Taunton Commission which reported in 1868, looked at smaller endowed and some private schools to complement Clarendon's work. With the future of endowed grammar schools being uncertain on the eve of the 1870 Education Act the Head Master of Uppingham founded the Headmasters' Conference in 1869 to convene an annual meeting to defend the schools' freedom. The government realised their significance, however, and the Endowed Schools Act (1869) broadened the curricula of such grammar schools, removed religious disabilities and made the governors more representative. The nine Public Schools recognised by Clarendon joined the Headmasters' Conference in 1870 and today 200, mostly independent and all now termed Public Schools belong to this Conference. The rich information found in records and registers maintained by the majority of schools in this category has been described above.

In the final third of the nineteenth century the child population in England increased boundlessly and British industry in a competitive world market was demanding better educated recruits. The educational facilities provided by the voluntary societies in England were inadequate for the demands of the century; thus in 1870, after considerable debate, W E Forster's Elementary Education Act for England and Wales was passed; see Chapter 13 for the Education (Scotland) Act of 1872. Forster had considerable insight into educational thought as his father-in-law was Thomas Arnold of Rugby School fame and his brother-in-law, Matthew Arnold was one of the first Inspectors appointed in 1869. Forster's Act obliged local authorities to establish rate-aided Board Schools in their areas if the numbers of existing voluntary schools were deemed inadequate. Locally elected Boards of between five and fifteen members were set up to manage these Board Schools and to raise finance for their operation by schools fees, by local rates, and by central government grants. The fees were the subject of much controversy and were not charged in many cases, the money being found by additional local taxation or rate levies. These were reduced in 1891 and finally abolished in elementary education in 1918. The Act also empowered, but did not compel, School Boards to make bylaws requiring parents to send their children of between 5 and 13 years to school. There was some confusion in the administering of the Act as the School Board areas were not always contiguous with the local authority areas, and the County Councils which eventually took over responsibility for primary and secondary education in England in 1902 were not themselves established until 1888. Nevertheless, records of the Boards and their schools are voluminous, some being held locally and others with the government's education departmental and ministry archives. A useful article by R B Pugh on sources for the histories of these schools appeared in the first volume of the 'British Journal of Educational Studies' in 1952.

Philanthropic endowments continued during this period: the boarding school for blind children in Sheffield built with money from a local bequest in 1870 is a typical example. Education of blind adults and children had initially been addressed in the previous century. At a School for the Blind instituted in Liverpool in 1791 its annual report for 1808 not only named its committee and subscribers (and listed their donations) but referred to similar schools in London, Edinburgh, Bristol and Norwich. The annual reports of schools such as this sometimes give names of pupils, their ages, their places of origin, the causes of their blindness and the subjects they were taught which included music and crafts. In many cases their subsequent employment, or demise, is identified. These schools were maintained by further donations or collections made by "Lady Collectors" who also were identified by name in the annual reports. A Society for Supplying Home Teachers and Books to Enable the Blind to Read, which advocated the Moon System had offices in Leith and Liverpool.

However, the central government pressed on with its legislation, some politicians believing that schools should provide not only education but free milk and meals. Other felt that parents, having produced the children, should be responsible for feeding, clothing and disciplining them, and not use a philanthropic education system as an excuse to relax, or even abandon, parental responsibilities. Sandon's Act of 1876 forbade the employment of children under 10 and made half-time attendance at school compulsory between the ages of 10 and 14. On the other hand a child who had passed Standard IV, or alternatively had a certain number of attendances each year during the preceding five years, could be exempted from further attendance. The latter "qualification" for exemption was disparagingly termed a Dunce's Pass. The 1880 Mundella Education Act attempted to regularise the situation by insisting that education was compulsory to the age of 13 although certain exemptions could apply to children over the age of 10. The clause in the 1876 Act on half-time schooling to the age of 14 was not repealed and so a child of 13 could leave on attendance alone - although children over 10, whose parents applied for exemption from the terms of the Act, could also leave. The age at which exemption applied was raised to 11 in 1893 and to 12 in 1899. As the decade progressed higher elementary schools were established - although there was some concern about the competition of these with the grammar schools. A Royal (the Cross) Commission on Elementary Education reported in 1888 on this competition and also discussed the philosophy of payment by results. Grants were subsequently given to provide teachers for specific projects - the teaching of science or drawing or cookery - or the better instruction of pupil teachers - or employing organising masters or additional local inspectors.

Technical Schools and Colleges were established after the Technical Instruction Act of 1889, thus providing vocational training - although as explained in Chapter 7 above, some Mechanics' Institutes had been formed from 1823 and the Factory and Colliery Schools and several other Industrial Schools, Railway Schools and Chemical Works Schools had been in existence before the middle of the century. In addition, the City and Guilds of London Institute had its roots in 1878; its subsequent history is outlined in Chapter 10 below. In Junior Technical Schools children were admitted at 13 and left at 16, having been prepared for a particular industry or industries; whereas in the majority of Technical Schools pupils entered at 16. Whether such institutions provided secondary education was never finally resolved, even during debates in the 1920s.

An interesting aspect of vocational training was provided in Northampton in 1896 when the county council established 'The Northamptonshire Domestic Economy School'. This was a boarding school for 30 girls who received instruction in dressmaking, cookery, laundry, needlework and housewifery. Although termed a school the Principal was designated a Superintendent, not a Head Mistress.

The Free Education Act 1891 endorsed the 1870 Act but provided for consideration to be given to school hours to enable the two hours compulsory attendance to be accommodated around the children's working hours.

As described already, a committee of the Privy Council had been responsible for those aspects of education where the State had intervened since 1839, and in 1856 was termed the Education Department; but in 1899 The Board of Education was created to assume the duties of that committee. In 1902 the former responsibilities of the School Boards were appropriated by the councils of boroughs or urban districts; Council Schools thus emerged from the Board Schools. From this date a list of all such ("elementary") schools containing enormous detail was published annually. As the buildings for the Council Schools were provided by the local authorities they, in some areas, were termed Provided Schools whilst the voluntary schools became known as Non-Provided Schools. The 1902 Act also enabled councils to establish

Continuation Schools to offer instruction to children for a number of years after leaving an elementary school. The instruction, normally for two hours on three evenings a week - though there were some Day Continuation Schools - was in subjects related to the individuals' work; i.e. pupils in industry were taught subjects such as science and workshop practice whilst those in commerce were taught English and mathematics. Both Day and Evening Continuation Schools also accepted adults. This concept was not new, however, for the Mechanics' Institutes founded 100 years earlier by Birkbeck and Brougham were a form of continuation education and the government had made funds available from 1851, as mentioned above. Working Men's Colleges were opened in 1899 in London (Toynbee Hall) and Oxford (Ruskin College); and in 1903 the Workers' Education Association was founded to provide classes around the country for adults - the classes at that time being taught by university lecturers.

The school leaving age was raised to 14 and the half-time system ended by the Education Act of 1918, which has thus coincidently but fortuitously increased the breadth of information available to the social historian, family historian, biographer and genealogist in a variety of school records.

Even after the 1870, 1872 and later Education Acts, philanthropists continued to contribute towards the education and well-being of British children. A typical example was Cyril Arthur Pearson, the newspaper magnate, who launched his Fresh Air Fund nationwide in 1892 to pay for city children to go on day trips into the countryside air, based on his successes in taking children from the East End of London to Epping Forest. Schools throughout the country applied for assistance from this fund which in many cases was used to encourage the pupils in their attendance and performance. Thus the children's diligence as well as their health was improved, as the outings were used as rewards. The enterprise continues to this day as Pearson's Holiday Fund being administered by the Shaftesbury Society.

9. British Academies Overseas

Reference has already been made to the universities which were established in Europe around the time of the Reformation for the education of those whose faith did not conform with that of the Established Church. There were, however, many other British educational academies, mostly schools, set up around the world in successive centuries to satisfy the needs of the British as they ventured abroad on a semi-permanent basis. The grand-tour of the gentry, of the literary class, of artists, and even of the fidgety, in the late eighteenth and the nineteenth centuries followed an established pattern with communities of Britons peppered across the globe. In many of these communities schools were opened in which the teaching was in English, following the curricula of the schools at home. There were, in addition, permanent settlements of the British elsewhere overseas where particular industries or trading posts had been founded. In several of these settlements schools were set up for the education in the English language of the children of the settlers, replicating the lessons that would have been learned in Victorian and Edwardian Britain. Welshmen took their families, as well as their mining skills, to a number of South American countries. Welsh-speaking communities, which encouraged schooling in Welsh, were established and flourished in the nineteenth century on that continent.

In a number of cases these schools remain today even though the British community has long since departed, and the buildings are now used for the exclusive education of the present locals. The records of the former British establishment may survive locally, even at the school, or in the local museum or archive, or have been brought to the British Isles. If the latter is the case even a tenuous link with the overseas community or venture may reveal the present location of the records. If the school was sustained by a particular religious denomination that body's historical society may hold the records. The Anglican churches overseas came under the Bishop of London whose records are at the Guildhall Library, London. The Colonial and Dominions

Office (and subsequently the Foreign Office) papers have been deposited at the Public Record Office, Kew, and it is possible that the required records may be found there, particularly if they were originally among the British Consulate's documents. The 'Current Guide to the Contents of the Public Record Office', available at Kew and Chancery Lane and also on microfiche in some other repositories should be consulted.

A typical example of an English school overseas is Heidelberg College, mentioned in the Preface, co-founded in 1887 by an Englishman, A B Catty and a German, Dr Albert Holzberg. This school was organised very much on the lines of an English public school with rowing and rugby football being as important as the academic subjects. The majority of the pupils entered British universities and the British or Indian Civil Service. The connections with England were severed during the 1914-18 War, but re-established in the 1930s, only to be finally ended during the Second World War. Records of former pupils and teachers can be found in copies of the school magazine, newspapers and journals in England and in Germany, and with descendants of former staff and pupils.

10. Awarding Bodies

Over the years there have been not a few bodies which have awarded accolades in one form or another for educational achievement or competency but not necessarily offering tuition. Some of these bodies are identified here; whilst not providing teaching themselves such bodies did, and indeed still do, generate extensive records of academic achievement or competence which are of value to the family historian and the biographer. The external degrees awarded by the University of London have already been mentioned in Chapter 4 above. The Union of Lancashire and Cheshire [Mechanics] Institutes had started a scheme of examinations in 1847 and the Union of Educational Institutions was formed in 1895 to serve the Midlands and South West of England. In fact by 1911 there were 40 external examining bodies; but perhaps the best known is the City and Guilds of London Institute established in 1878 by the Corporation of London and fourteen of the City Livery Companies. In 1880 it was given its full title of City and Guilds of London Institute for the Advancement of Technical Education, by which time two other Companies were contributing. It provided immediate financial assistance to City of London schools and colleges, at Finsbury for example, but built its own premises - the Central Institute - in South Kensington in 1884. This changed its name to City and Guilds College in 1908 when it combined with the Royal College of Science (founded in 1845) and the Royal School of Mines to form Imperial College of the University of London. The City and Guilds of London Art School, originally acquired by the Institute in 1878 as the Lambeth School of Art, became another of the Institute's colleges until it broke away in 1971. From this date although the Institute continued to make appointments to the Governing Body of Imperial College, it had become exclusively an examining and awarding body and was concentrating on craft skills. Its certificates are renowned world-wide for the standards they signify, and are thus an important class of educational record.

Even more recent are the Business and Technology Education Council

(BTEC) and the National Council for Vocational Qualifications (NCVQ) which award, or authorise the awarding of, certificates at various levels to signify particular academic achievements or work-based competences.

The professional scientific and engineering institutions such as the Royal Society of Chemistry, the Institution of Mechanical Engineers, and the Institute of Energy, all founded in the nineteenth and early twentieth centuries, have awarded certificates and medals to their members who have attained certain professional standards of competency, academically, practically and managerially. Such professional bodies have maintained libraries and records of their members which in some cases may be consulted by the serious historian and biographer, occasionally on payment of a fee. The standards of the larger institutions have been upheld through the Engineering Council which is also an awarding body bestowing the status of Chartered Engineer, Incorporated Engineer or Engineering Technician as appropriate. The records of this body are equally useful to the historical researcher.

Other professional awarding bodies are those connected with the medical profession, such as the Royal College of Physicians, and the Royal College of Surgeons whose records stretch back well into the nineteenth century. Many of these records and registers have been published in book form and are available in the larger public libraries throughout the British Isles and in university libraries elsewhere in the English-speaking world.

Veterinary surgeons, accountants, auditors, actuaries, and surveyors each have their own body which has made awards for achieving a specific educational, academic or practical standard of competence. The needs of the arts have been met by bodies such as the Royal Academy of Music, the Royal College of Organists and the Royal Society of Arts which over the years have awarded certificates, medals and other trophies for academic and practical achievement. The addresses of all these bodies are to be found in educational publications such as the 'World of Learning' and in current telephone directories.

11. Establishment-based School Records

Any documents extant for the Monastic or Chantry Schools prior to the sixteenth century are likely to be found in the Public Record Office, London, or in rare cases at diocesan or county record offices. Deeds relating to the foundation of this type of school long after this period as well, in fact into the present century, were enrolled in Chancery and so appear in the Close Rolls from 1204 until 1903. From this time onwards such deeds were enrolled in the Supreme Court, and so appear in the Enrolment Books of that Court. Printed or typescript copies of the earlier and even the later material should be sought initially, and there are indexes to the trust deeds in the Public Record Office for the period from 1736 to 1904 at Chancery Lane, London. For locally deposited material the local county archivist will be able to advise on its availability.

The schoolmasters' licences referred to above from the local bishop or his representative have not survived in vast quantities; some are in diocesan and parochial archives, now in county record offices, others are in the Exchequer records at the Public Record Office. The records of the teachers having subscribed to the Thirty Nine Articles are in the Bishops' Subscription Books, also in the diocesan archives. Besides the name of a master and his status, these records also detail the type of school and its method of support by fees or endowment.

Information on Charity Schools from the seventeenth and eighteenth centuries can be found in the 1819 Report of the Brougham Commission, which was actually set up to examine the wider aspects of charities. The SPCK Reports list those schools which that Society had founded and supported by charity.

The registers and records of the Headmasters' Conference Schools and Public Schools and their founding institutions have already been recommended as valuable sources of information on both boys and masters; Dr Jacobs' list of

Registers referred to in Chapter 4 should be consulted. Many of these registers and the schools histories, having been printed and published, are quite easily consulted by family and social historians and genealogists. The series of articles by W E Tate 'Some Sources for the History of English Grammar Schools' which was published in the British Journal of Educational Studies in 1953/4, although more concerned with schools than pupils, merits consultation.

Schools records for the village-based institutions, whether Dame Schools, Charity Schools, British Schools, National Schools or Board Schools, in many cases are still retained at the school, or are with the county Education Authorities, or have been deposited in county record offices or with the original supporting body. Unfortunately not a few of these unique records have been found so interesting by some teachers that to do research more conveniently the records have been taken from the schools and have not yet been returned. Records for the town and city-based schools may be at the schools or in city or borough record offices or libraries, in town halls, borough education offices, museums or with the county archivists.

The SPCK archives at Holy Trinity Church, Marylebone Road, London NW1 4DU contain many references to the Charity Schools in which the SPCK took an interest, but its coordination role was not very thorough; although there were annual 'Accounts' from 1704 with lists of schools, much of the information outside the Home Counties was not updated annually. Whilst considerable correspondence is held centrally there is often very much more detail on individual schools in local record offices.

Schools connected to the Established Church of England (and so originally associated with the National Schools) either have retained their records at the school or with the local clergyman or have deposited them with the Diocesan Registrar; in the latter case the documents will now be in the county record office, having been sent direct to the ecclesiastical authorities or kept with the parochial material in the Parish Chest and subsequently deposited. The route by which the school records arrived in the county archives may influence the way in which they are catalogued. Some of the National Schools' documents are deposited at the Church of England Record Centre at 15 Galleywall Road, London SE16 3PB. The Society's Reports, particularly in the early nineteenth century, including indexed registers of teachers trained at their Central School from 1812 to 1851 and Admissions Registers for their training colleges at Chelsea (1841-48) and Battersea (1844-48), are valuable sources of detail on their own schools. The National Society published a 'Monthly Paper' from 1847 to 1875 which became the 'School Guardian' until 1937; copies of these are available for research.

The schools supported by other groups such as Jews, Quakers, Independents (Congregationalists), Baptists, Presbyterians, Moravians, Methodists or Unitarians may have deposited their records with their own Historical or Record Societies, or in Dr Williams' Library collection at the Public Record Office, London, or at the local county record office, or they may still hold the records at the schools themselves. The early annual reports of the British School Society from 1806 and the 'Quarterly Extracts' (1827-1848) from the correspondence of the Society, which was superseded by the 'Educational Record' until 1929, contain details on their own schools to which many dissenting Protestants sent their children in England, Wales and Scotland. The most useful report is that for 1897 as it contains a list of almost all the British Schools which ever existed, although some of the data is not totally correct. In general, however, there is less information available in the reports after 1870 when the School Boards took over responsibility for many of the British Schools. In preparing its formal submission to the Newcastle Commission in 1861 the British Society collected comprehensive information from its grant-aided schools. This information in the form of returns is today filed by counties in the Society archives. Amongst its correspondence are communications from some ragged schools, orphanages, and small private schools and there are also some prospectuses from a range of these schools. The British and Foreign School Society Archives Centre, which also holds some school log and minutes books, is in the West London Institute of Higher Education, Borough Road, Isleworth, Middlesex, TW7 5DU. The British Schools annual reports from 1814 are available on microfiche and may be purchased commercially.

In the Jewish Schools identified above in Chapter 2 each boy, after 1811, had to submit a certificate from the Mohel stating his age before he was granted admission. The 'Manuscript Minutes Book of the Talmud Torah 1791-1818' in particular, and various articles in the 'Jewish Chronicle', the 'Voice of Jacob' and the 'Jewish World' are rich sources of information on the school and the achievements in English and Hebrew of its pupils, who were rewarded

with silver medals. The activities of other schools, such as the West Metro-
politan Jewish School (founded in 1845) and those in Stepney, Bayswater
and Borough (founded in the 1860s), are reported in these publications. The
Jewish Historical Society of England at 33 Seymour Place, London W1H
5AP may advise on the whereabouts of this material. The schools established
by Christians for Jewish children in the East End of London, as described in
Chapter 2, must not be overlooked. Hence records of the education of Jewish
children should be sought in Christian school archives if a search in Jewish
material proves fruitless.

The activities of the Catholic Poor School Committee, mentioned in Chapter
2 above, may be followed by studying its annual reports from 1848, held by
the Catholic Education Council at 41 Cromwell Road, London SW7 2DJ.
The 1845 survey of Catholic Schools is contained in the second (1849) report.
These reports are also available on microfiche. The Committee's periodical
'The Catholic School' has many names that researchers may find useful.

The Friends' Schools for Quakers' children founded in 1815 at Wigton in
Cumberland and in 1825 at Croydon in Surrey (but moving in 1879 to Saffron
Walden in Essex), and for boys only at Bootham School, York, being
substantial schools have all published their registers. Smaller schools and
Adult Schools supported by Quakers have been mentioned in earlier chapters
of this Cameo; their records may have been deposited in county archives,
although the Society of Friends at Friends House, Euston Road, London NW1
2BJ may be able to assist with additional information.

For the Wesleyan Committee of Education the annual reports from 1837 to
1932 are held at the Methodist Church Division of Education and Youth at
2 Chester House, Pages Lane, Muswell Hill, London N10 1P2. Comprehensive data in tabular form on numbers of schools, teachers, and pupils appeared
in almost every annual report; and many reports contain names of the teachers
in day and Sunday schools. There are also indexed extracts from the reports
from 1850.

The Ragged School Union annual reports from 1844, and its magazine with
various titles from 1848 to the present day, are held by the Shaftesbury
Society at 18-20 Kingston Road, London SW19 1JZ. The minutes books from
1844 for its organisational meetings in Scotland, as well as England are held
by the Society, and most are also available in microform.

It is possible that some or all of the records of the above schools, particularly the smaller institutions, were maintained by the proprietor or the Headmaster or Headmistress, and when those individuals moved on or retired the documents went with them. Thus many of the records have been lost, while others are even today being discovered from time to time and either returned to the school or placed in a suitable archive repository.

Where schools records survive, whatever the background or the supporting agency of the establishment, there are normally Registers with admission and withdrawal pages giving dates, ages, residences, the fathers' occupations and sometimes names and the means of previous education. In some of the voluntary schools' Admissions Registers there may even be a note of whether the child had been baptised or not. The reasons for leaving the school, which are often included, provide a vivid insight to the community as well as historical information on the child and his or her family. The school Log Book, a requirement in government financed schools from 1863, normally provides detail of attendance, accidents and illnesses of the staff and the children. It was in such a book that the commentary in the Preface on the author's grandmother was discovered. Noteworthy weather conditions and visits to the school, punishments and local celebrations, prizes and grants, inspectors' reports on discipline and competence of the teachers and the pupils are also given, often in descriptive detail. Reasons for absences of the children, such as harvests in rural communities or military victories in urban schools, or individual problems created by parents, pupils and teachers are described in illustrative writing - not because the teacher was demonstrating frustrated journalism but because the numbers of pupils attending the school affected the local grant it obtained and so it was important to record genuine reasons for low numbers. Accordingly the true personalities of all those concerned in the teaching and learning process can come alive by research into these log books. Log books have been in common use from about 1840 to the present day, even though in some schools they were not required until 1863. They are particularly graphic from 1860 to 1900 when the system of 'payment by results' was in vogue.

Candidates entered for examinations or assessments were recorded in separate books for that purpose at some schools; where this was the case the names of the candidates, their ages, how many attendances they made for the particular assessments, their standards and results were recorded. For some schools there were separate Punishment Books (apart from the usual Log Books) in which were entered the pupils' names, ages and on occasions addresses, the nature of the offences and the punishments meeted out. At the other end of the spectrum some schools had separate Medal Records (also apart from the Log Books) with details on the pupil, the cause being rewarded and the date of the medal being awarded; such medals (see Chapter 12) proliferated from 1907. There may have been separate Honours Books, or even Honours Boards, bearing the names of the honoured pupils, the events for which the pupils were being recognised and the relevant years.

Absenteeism, and local and statutory attempts to rectify it, created another series of records: there were letters from parents offering reasons for their child being absent, the Attendance Officer's report if the parents had to be taken to Court for their child's continued absences; there would be notes of the incentives of offering Attendance Medals and Certificates for regular or unbroken attendance, while the leaving records would note if the child had to leave the school under adverse circumstances.

There may be examples of the timetables and the teaching and learning aids such as reading primers which were designed not only to develop the children's reading skills but also to improve their moral standards.

The Minutes Books of the school managers, trustees and governors and of School Boards, if available, provide additional information sometimes on the pupils as well as the teachers and the members of the Boards themselves, and in some circumstances on Subscribers to the school. Such minutes with inventories, correspondence, and plans, drawings and photographs of the school building are often held in local education offices. Careful analysis of all this material will give sufficient detailed background to be able to fit the children precisely into their academic environment.

At the school there may be foundation stones or wall tablets inscribed with the date of opening or extension and the name or names of the dignitaries present at a formal unveiling ceremony. A picture can accordingly be built up of a particular school from its initial launching, even the advance planning needed before this, through its day-to-day operation, with information on the teachers as well as the pupils, and possibly the scale of fees charged.

Names, ages and birthplaces of pupils boarding at even small private institutions in the nineteenth century can be found in the decennial census returns; earlier population listings, as in the case of the school at Ealing in 1599, provide similar information. For a full description of these listings see the Chapmans Records Cameo 'Pre-1841 Censuses and Population Listings in the British Isles' published by Lochin.

Noteworthy events at a school such as a musical evening, a magic lantern show, a treat, an annual tea party, an anniversary or speech day may have been recorded by the local media. The jubilee celebrations for Macclesfield Sunday School in 1846 were so important that all the mills and workshops in the town closed for the day; the Macclesfield Courier reported that 3000 townsfolk waved off 2143 pupils and teachers on a train excursion to Stockport.

There are likely to be records surviving of the watch-dog body for a particular school such as Government Inspectors' reports for the state-linked schools and Diocesan Inspectors' reports for those schools linked to the Established Church. Other denominationally-linked schools had similar reports from their own inspectors. Even some Sunday Schools had Visitors appointed by the School Superintendent to overlook classes and supervise teachers, checking the attendance in their classes every five weeks. Although many of these records are bound to contain names and further details on the teachers, even their contracts, including pupil teachers, and possibly information on the hours of school work and the general conduct of the school affairs, there may be occasional references to individual pupils, the subjects of the biographer or the family historian.

In the nineteenth century there were several national surveys for Parliament on education and educational institutions. These, and the very many tables attached to them in appendices, furnish enormous detail county by county, even village by village in some cases, on the schools, their affiliations, numbers and sexes of pupils, salaries of teachers and if libraries were attached. The surveys of particular value are those of 1816, 1833, 1837/38 (which includes considerable detail on Northampton) and the 1851 Census of Education. The reports of the Royal Commissions of 1861 under Lord Clarendon and of 1868 under Lord Taunton examine secondary education in depth throughout England and Wales. The 1895 Report on Secondary Education on a county-by-county basis examines in minute detail even the social conditions within each school. The minutes of the Committee of the Privy Council identified above, which had been established in 1839 to deal with government grants for school buildings and many other organisational matters, offer information on individual schools.

The Royal Commission Reports were published as Parliamentary Papers, some of which were issued as Blue Books and indexed. Several of the Parliamentary Papers and some indexes have been reprinted by the Irish University Press. Some of the larger public libraries and many university libraries, particularly those with a faculty of education, have copies of either the original Papers, the Blue Books or the reprints.

For the present century there have been several reports for specific counties dealing with endowments for elementary education prior to the First World War - Northamptonshire in 1906, for example (1906, xc).

The Public Record Office holds a great deal of information (besides that mentioned above) on schools in the ED Class, although there is almost no detail on pupils' names. The following explanatory leaflets are available from the Public Record Office, Ruskin Avenue, Kew, Surrey, TW9 4DU:

- 77 - Records Relating to Elementary and Secondary Schools

- 78 - Education: Records of Teachers

- 79 - Education: Records of Special Services

- 80 - Records Relating to Technical and Further Education.

12. Pupil-based School Records

Besides the records retained by those who owned, supported, organised or managed the schools described above, certain documents and other artifacts were given by these establishments to the children or to their parents or guardians. Although often ignored in many works on school records these are frequently of greater value to the social and family historian than many of the establishment-based records so far mentioned. The pupil-based records are more difficult to locate, but for those undertaking genealogical or biographical research such material can often be found among papers, documents or souvenirs kept by the older members of a family. And whilst not tangible records, the recollections and reminiscences of these family members should be sought and noted with some urgency before their valuable oral historical contributions are lost forever. For notable local or national figures, their scholastic memorabilia may be displayed in museums or art galleries.

Items such as text books or readers used by the pupils give an immediate indication of the subjects and standards taught. Examination papers show the depth of knowledge expected of the children, undergraduates or adults. Exercise books, in an ancestor's or biographee's own handwriting, provide a guide to the information imparted, or more correctly, to the information received by the student. A picturesque alternative to an exercise book is a sampler, often beautifully hand-stitched by a child in the eighteenth or nineteenth century.

Reports indicate how much of each subject was understood, or at least retained for the particular term or year. Some school reports detail not only academic prowess but regularity of attendance, athletic ability, character and personality assessment and general health and potential. Height and weight, term by term, were stated on the report forms or in the report books issued by some schools. For those who achieved exceptional standards in the academic subjects, prizes, normally in the form of books with suitable bookplates or inscriptions, were frequently awarded. External examining bodies often also issued certificates of achievement. When the economic conditions of the school, the Church, the charity, the voluntary society or the local authority were limited, then certificates were issued in place of books. To encourage pupils who had little academic aptitude but who excelled in athletic achievement then medallions, plaques, cups, trophies and certificates were often awarded by the school. Many such an award was engraved with details of the prize and the date on which it had been attained. Some schools made awards for craftwork or at hobbies exhibitions and these may have survived to this day among family archives.

Before education became compulsory many schools encouraged their students by awarding attendance medals, honours cards and certificates. At least one school (at Usk in Monmouth) in the late eighteenth century gave 1/2d to the best boy of the week, which unfortunately will not be commemorated by any pupil-based records extant today; however, the same school gave the best-catechism boy a medal with riband in addition to the 1/2d, and such a prize may well have survived. Monitors at this school could earn 1/2d, 1d or 2d a week, but more important to the family historian today (though possibly not to the boys two hundred years ago !) those monitors were given merit tickets or books which are likely to have survived. Other medals and silk woven badges were issued to pupils to commemorate school anniversaries; having worn them for processions and parades the pupils were permitted to retain these souvenirs.

School attendance medals, in recent years, have attracted the attention of numismatists as well as educational and family historians. It is feasible, therefore, that medals awarded a hundred or more years ago which have passed out of a family can be retrieved through coin or medal dealers. Some county magazines and journals have occasional articles on medals awarded by specific schools, management committees, schools boards or education authorities for 'Superior Merit' and 'Good Conduct' as well as for 'Punctual', 'Regular', 'Full', 'Unbroken' 'Excellent' or 'Perfect Attendance'. Cedric Day's useful book 'School Attendance Medals of England, Scotland & Wales' published by Whitmore in 1992, gives a geographically alphabetical listing of many examples of these types of medals - with some details on the issuing authorities; this book also includes a brief mention of Sunday School medals.

From the middle of the nineteenth century many schools, from the tiny village establishment to the endowed school and the university, arranged for photographs to be taken of various groups. Posed by classes, by years, by sports teams or even panoramically of the entire school, many of these school photographs were given, or sold, to the students and their parents or guardians. Although those found in private hands may be unmarked and have no indication of who is who, it is worth checking with the school or among the school-based records (which today could be in a record office) to see if they have retained similar or even identical photographs but with every individual named.

Sandon's 1876 Elementary Education Act required children who left school, either before the statutory leaving age or after attaining Standard IV, to be given a School Leaving Certificate. Standard forms of this document, popularly called a Labour Certificate, were not introduced until 1901. After the passing of the 1918 Education Act the use of this certificate was discontinued. Because the school leaving age was gradually raised by exemption clauses in the various Education Acts of 1876, 1880, 1893, 1899 and finally in 1918, these Labour Certificates do not all bear exactly comparable information. However, the details on the documents do provide interesting data on the pupils, their dates of birth and their academic abilities.

The achievements, both academic and athletic, of the students at many educational establishments from the close of the eighteenth century to this day have been reported in local and national newspapers and specialist magazines and journals. Many of the reports, especially in more recent times include photographs. Whilst these publications and cuttings from them are perhaps more correctly described as establishment-based, in very cases the pupils themselves or their parents or guardians collected copies with a personal interest and so may be found today in family archives with pupil-based material. Some egocentric enthusiasts even compiled scrapbooks of newspaper cuttings on themselves and their friends' educational achievements; hopefully such a scrapbook has survived for your subject.

Some academic institutions or their Old Boys' or Old Girls' Associations have held regular, often annual, reunions of their former students. In some cases these were accompanied by a formal dinner for which a menu with the names of the principal guests as well as the food dishes were printed. It was the tradition at many such dinners for those attending to collect the autographs of their former class-mates. Documents with such personal connections could easily be disposed of as of no possible interest to the present generation when a family member dies; but for the true family historian even a menu card can divulge a treasure-chest of information.

Many school children, undergraduates and adult scholars kept diaries, pocket-books or journals of their personal activities, including their student days and recorded their relationships with their friends and reactions to matters educational. Such accounts penned by the subject of your research may have survived; or possibly he or she, or the institution attended are mentioned in the writings of a local diarist whose manuscript has been deposited in the county record office or whose work has even been published and is thus available in a public library.

Illustration to Vanity Fair. Engraving by
Thackery.

13. Scottish Education Records

Although much of the content of the preceding chapters is relevant to all of the British Isles some matters of detail are specific to Scotland and are thus elaborated upon in this chapter. A major distinction of Scottish education was the deep interest of town, burgh or parish councils in the education of local children at both primary and secondary level - in fact in providing at the parochial level all the necessary scholastic skills for the receptive pupils, whatever their social background, to equip them for tertiary education at a university.

Reference has already been made to Scottish universities and their alumni records and Dr Jacobs' work includes notes on these; but the appointments of academic staff from 1660 to 1898 may be found in Privy Seal English [this indicates the records were written in English] records (PS.3) in the Scottish Record Office (SRO); and references to their salaries may be located in Exchequer records E.224, 313, 810 and 811.

The 'Biographical Dictionary of Scottish Graduates to AD 1410' by Donald E R Watt, published in 1977, whilst not dealing with tertiary or higher education in Scotland, does offer in a unique form details on Scottish students who attended universities in Paris, Orleans, Bologna, Oxford and Cambridge.

Anderson's University was the colloquial name for the scientific institution and library founded with the bequest in 1796 of John Anderson, a professor at Glasgow University. In 1912 Anderson's became Glasgow's Royal Technical College, but over a century earlier it had kindled George Birkbeck's interest in teaching technicians and mechanics.

Independent school records in Scotland are likely to be at the schools themselves, although those for George Heriot's Schools, Edinburgh are in the SRO in the GD.421 series, as are those from 1854 for Dr Guthrie's Schools for destitute children (in the GD.425 series). Some of the Grammar Schools have published registers and details on their pupils and in some cases their later lives; such material is, therefore, available through any public library to all researchers. A typical example is the 1923 work on Aberdeen Grammar School registers from 1796. Dr Jacobs' booklet should be consulted for references to such material.

Many burgh or town councils in Scotland took an active interest in the education of their local children even in the fifteenth century, establishing Lecture Schools to teach reading and writing; whereas in England such interest was shown only by the Church at this time. In fact the Scottish burghs came into conflict with, and won against, the Church on this very matter; as a consequence Burgh Schools, such as that in Peebles in 1464, became established with the town councils very much in control of the curriculum and payment of teachers. An Act of Parliament in 1496 required all barons and freeholders of substance to send their eldest sons to a Grammar School at 8 or 9 years of age until they had mastered "perfect Latin" and then to a School of Art and Law for three years. But as so few records have survived for this pattern of education it is doubtful if the Act was enforced, even for the wealthier classes.

At the Reformation John Knox's 'First Book of Discipline' advocated in 1560 that there should be a school in every parish or associated with every kirk (church) - with parents paying for their children if they could afford it, or supported by the Church if not. The plan was to establish Grammar Schools, and even Higher Grammar Schools, in notable towns throughout Scotland, the costs being found as in England from the dissolution of the monasteries by the 1548 Chantries Act. But, as in England, the cash did not reach the schools and Knox's plans could not be fulfilled. However, his aspirations were not lost and his idea that the Church should assist in the education of poor children caused the burghs to withdraw their animosity. As a consequence when the 1616 and 1696 Acts were passed requiring a school to be established in every parish in Scotland the town councils and the Church cooperated closely and Primary Schools were opened in Scotland over 200 years ahead of England. This resulted in many schoolteachers, until 1939, being appointed in Scotland on a parochial basis, nominated by the landowner (heritor) and parish minister and approved by the presbytery following an interview. Accordingly, the teachers' names appear in the Heritors' Records and in the presbytery minutes books. Kirk sessions' records often also furnish schoolteachers' names as the presbytery may merely have ratified the decision of a kirk session. It is possible that the burgh or town council discussed the appointment of a burgh schoolteacher, in which case the teacher's name will appear in the council minutes.

A Parliamentary Commission of 1690 reviewed education; its report includes lists of schoolmasters in Angus, Ayrshire, Berwickshire, East Lothian, Fife, Midlothian, Peeblesshire, Perthshire, Roxburghshire and Stirlingshire. Apart from Ayrshire these lists were published in 1965 by the Scottish History Society in their 4th series, Volume 2 - 'Miscellany'.

The Society in Scotland for Propagating Christian Knowledge (SSPCK) undertook similar projects in the eighteenth and nineteenth centuries, particularly in the "Highlands, Islands and Remote Corners", to those of its English counterpart - the SPCK. The school on St Kilda is one of the earliest SSPCK Schools, and the Spinning School established at Stornoway in 1763 was largely the result of SSPCK efforts. Contrary to the policy of the government, the SSPCK encouraged the teaching of Gaelic in its schools. By the early 1800s there were 16,000 pupils in 290 SSPCK Schools. The philanthropic movements described in Chapter 7 above were equally active in Scotland: a Ragged School for boys was opened in Aberdeen in 1841, for girls in 1843 and a mixed ragged school in 1845, around the time that the London Ragged School Union was formed. The records of the SSPCK are in the GD.95/7, /8 and /9 series in the SRO and include school registers (from 1710), salary books (from 1766) and school returns (from 1827).

Mutual Benefit Societies were formed by teachers in Glasgow in 1794, in Roxburgh in 1811 and in Jedburgh in 1824. The archives of these have been deposited with those of the Educational Institute mentioned below.

An Education Act of 1803 which applied only to rural areas of Scotland, determined wages, incidentally higher than hitherto, for the parish schoolmasters. As with the 1616 and 1696 Acts (see above) the heritors were very much involved and in conjunction with the parish ministers were now to appoint the schoolmasters. In many cases the heritors paid the masters' salaries. In the very remote parts such as the Highlands and Western Islands where the parishes covered vast geographical areas, an additional building, called a Side School, was needed in which to teach the children; the heritors suitably adjusted their financial outlays.

An important benefactor for schooling in Aberdeenshire, Banffshire and Morayshire was James Dick who set up a Trust for the maintenance and assistance of parochial schoolmasters in these counties. From 1832 names of masters who benefited are in the Trust archives at the SRO (GD.1/4 series).

The Highland Schools Act of 1838 required funds to be made available from the Treasury for further schools in the Highlands. As a result Highland teachers are named in the Exchequer Records (E.224/32-40), especially from 1840 to 1863.

The Free Church of Scotland, founded in 1843, encouraged its churches to establish their own schools and appoint their own teachers. The Deacons' Courts' minutes of those church records give names of the teachers.

The Educational Institute of Scotland - a professional association of teachers - was founded in 1847. The records of the names of its members have been deposited (series GD.342) in the SRO with the archives of the Mutual Benefit Societies mentioned above.

School Inspectors' reports for 1859 and 1866/67 are in the (indexed) ED.16/13 and 16/14 series at the SRO. These reports name teachers, pupil teachers and some assistant teachers for a selection of Scottish schools.

The Education (Scotland) Act of 1872, more embracing than Forster's Elementary Education Act for England and Wales, made provision for School Boards to administer education at all levels by parishes. The minutes books of these Boards are now with county council archives at the SRO or in the appropriate local record offices and libraries in Scotland. The reports of School Inspectors for the Scottish Education Department from 1896 in the ED.16-18 series are, in general, less informative than their English counterparts. The Leaving Certificates registers (ED.36) from 1908 give details on each pupil but are closed to public inspection for 75 years. The certificates themselves may have survived in private hands and form similar pupil-based records to those described above in Chapter 12.

Industrial and Reformatory Schools, as in England and Wales, were established in Scotland from the nineteenth century. For example, the Dundee Industrial Schools for Girls was founded in 1846, its records being still at the school. There were also Reformatory Ships, the Cumberland being moored off Helensburgh, Dumbarton from 1869 until it was subject to an arson attack in 1889. It was replaced by the Empress in the following year and housed 400 boys. The Mars, which also held 400 boys, was moored off Dundee from 1869 until 1929 and this had additional accommodation in its tender, the Lightning.

The 'Royal (Argyle) Commission to Inquire into Schools in Scotland' whose report appeared as Parliamentary Papers (from 1865 to 1868, xvii, xxv, xxvi, and xxix) was the Scottish equivalent to the Clarendon Commission, but covered a wider range of types of schools than the English and Welsh survey.

The addresses of the extant educational institutions mentioned above may be found in current telephone directories; the Scottish Record Office is located at HM General Register House, Edinburgh, EH1 1YY, Scotland.

14. Irish Education Records

Similarly to Scottish material, many of the comments in this Cameo apply in general terms equally to Ireland. The very early Irish centres of teaching and learning were mentioned in Chapters 2 and 3. A register of the students and graduates of Trinity College (Dublin University) from 1593 to 1846 was published as 'Alumni Dublinenses' with a supplement from 1846 to 1860 in its second edition by George Dames Burtchaell and Thomas Ulick Sadleir in 1935. There had earlier been a 'Catalogue of Graduates who have Proceeded to Degrees in the University of Dublin' from 1591 to 1868, prepared by Charles Miller and published in 1869 with subsequent volumes to 1895, 1931, 1952 and 1969. Queen's University in Belfast, though considerably younger, has similar alumni information available, as does the National University of Ireland with its colleges at Cork, Galway, Maynooth and Dublin. The grammar school at Derry, formerly called the Londonderry Free Grammar School and established in the seventeenth century, has had its registers of pupils from 1617 to 1814 published, as has Kilkenny School from 1685 to 1800 by Thomas Sadleir who worked on the Dublin University alumni material.

The Irish Inns of Court have already been mentioned in Chapter 4, but in the Admissions Papers for those apprentices who were to become attorneys in Ireland, statements on their previous education had to made and affidavits signed where necessary. Similarly for barristers, their previous education in terms of location, subjects and achievement was recorded in the students' admissions papers.

Several schools with independent means have published lists and registers of their pupils and their subsequent careers and so can be obtained through public or university libraries. These schools and the Irish Universities appear in Dr Jacobs' booklet. Charity Schools may have had their registers published; The Blue Coat School founded at Cork in 1780 and better known as St Stephen's Hospital, is one such school for which the registers are available.

There are no such lists for the Hedge Schools but the Irish National Archives at Bishop Street, Dublin 8, Ireland hold much educational archival material.

The Kildare Place Society was formed in 1811 to provide nondenominational education for the poor, and whilst no religious teaching should have taken place, the Authorised Version of the Bible was used as a reading book. The Society also established Training and Model Schools in Dublin, but having few funds persuaded the London government to provide £7000 in 1815 and from 1817 an annual grant of ultimately £30,000. This enabled the Society to extend its activities into publishing school textbooks for use in England as well as in Ireland. However, the Catholic Church did not believe the teaching was nondenominational and opposed the use of the Authorised Version, advocating the Douai Version of the Bible. To satisfy its critics the Society appointed paid inspectors in 1820; by 1825 the Society had divided Ireland into eight school areas each with its own inspector, two being Catholic. The inspectors' reports to the Society's headquarters provide valuable information on these schools. But the Catholic Church was still not satisfied and a Commission of Enquiry was set up that year which also published a useful report. Whilst the report was favourable, a Select Committee of the House of Commons in 1829 advocated complete secular education. This resulted in the Kildare Place Society losing its grant and in 1831 a Board of Commissioners of National Education in Ireland being established, on which all denominations were represented, to oversee an unsectarian system. The eight areas already delineated were used, but now half of the inspectors were Catholic. Neither the Authorised nor the Douai Versions of the Bible were permitted in the schools, only biblical abstracts prepared by the Commission. The first report of the National Board appeared in 1834. Select Committees of the House of Commons on the Progress and Organisation of the New Plan of Education in Ireland reported in 1835 and 1837 on the situations in these schools, mostly reflecting disagreements between teachers and Board inspectors. The latter paid unannounced visits to the schools but as the teachers always managed to discover their plans, the centrally based inspectors were replaced with 25 local people. This experience was drawn heavily upon when establishing the School Inspectorate in England and Wales in 1839 - which also accounts for the unpopularity of its introduction in England.

The report (PP.1826-27.xii) of an Irish Education Inquiry undertaken in 1824 includes details under provinces, by counties, on 46 Female Schools attached to Nunneries, 352 Roman Catholic Day Schools, and on schools in connection with the Kildare Place Society (over 1000), the London Hibernian Society (618), the Association for Discounting Vice (226), the Trustees of Erasmus Smith (113), the Baptist Society (88) and many other organisations accounting for a total of 11,823 schools with 12,530 teachers and 560,549 scholars, compared with 4,600 schools and 200,000 scholars in 1811 (PP.1813-14.v). There are tables and lists of schools with addresses, if they are free or Pay [many Hedge] Schools, the material of their construction (eg mud and thatch, stone and lime etc), the numbers of pupils, if the scriptures are read, and extremely usefully, the name, religion and income of the teacher. The Parliamentary Papers also include some Inspectors' Reports stating names and ages of teachers and referring to registers, reports and class lists being kept.

15. Valete

The preceding chapters have indicated the growth of Education in Britain during a period of just over 1000 years. Records are extant of schools and other academic institutions throughout that period although their value to the social and family historian, the biographer and the genealogist varies enormously.

Some documents are packed with names and biographical details of the pupils and students while other material contains only the tutors, teachers, instructors and lecturers. The earliest records tend to be deposited in the Public Record Office while the later material can be found at the school, academy or university with the supporting organisation or in the Scottish Record Office, the Irish National Archives, in Diocesan or County Record Offices or similar local repositories.

In every instance potential researchers are advised to contact the repository well in advance of a proposed visit, to ascertain the availability of records and research facilities.

Mementos of instruction and possibly achievement may have been awarded to the pupil and retained in national, local or private custody. Whatever the material, education records can paint a picture of an individual, perhaps an ancestor, providing not only his portrait but also a backdrop of his religious, political, social and economic life and environment.

Index